Along the Way

Along the Way

Building a Legacy
That
Changes Lives

Lynette Hagin

16 15 14 13 12 11 10   07 06 05 04 03 02 01

Along the Way: Building a Legacy That Changes Lives
ISBN 13: 978-0-89276-807-3
ISBN 10: 0-89276-807-X

In the U.S. write:
Kenneth Hagin Ministries
P.O. Box 50126
Tulsa, OK 74150-0126
1-888-28-FAITH
www.rhema.org

In Canada write:
Kenneth Hagin Ministries
P.O. Box 335, Station D
Etobicoke (Toronto), Ontario
Canada, M9A 4X3
1-866-70-RHEMA
www.rhemacanada.org

Contents

———⚬———

INTRODUCTION

God has given each and every one of us an amazing opportunity to make a difference in the lives of those around us. In some cases, we can make a difference for eternity. I have a powerful story to share with you that illustrates what I'm talking about here.

One morning a father and son were walking along a beach when they came upon a stunning sight. Countless starfish had washed up during the night when the tide was high. The helpless starfish were still moving, still alive, and still clamoring to try to get back into the ocean.

The father and son knew it wouldn't be long until the sun would bake the poor creatures trapped there on the sand. There were thousands of them, as far as the eye could see.

The little boy leaned down and scooped up a starfish, flinging it like a Frisbee out into the ocean. He repeated the process over and over again, trying to save as many of the creatures as possible.

Once the father realized what his little boy was doing, he felt it was his parental duty to teach him a harsh life lesson. So he said, "Son, what you're doing here is noble, but you can't save all of these starfish. There are thousands of them. The sun is getting really hot. They're going to die."

The son didn't say anything at first. Instead, he just stared at his daddy. Next he carefully picked up another starfish and flung it out into the ocean as far as he could. Then he slowly replied, "Well, I just made all the difference in the world for that one."

Jesus said in Matthew 10:29, "Isn't a human life worth more than many sparrows" (or starfish)? You and I may not be able to lead thousands of people to the Lord, but we can lead just one. We can make all the difference for one.

How can we make a difference? By developing a legacy that will lead someone to the Lord. Whether we realize it or not, the people around us are watching us. The legacy we write will either lead them to Jesus or drive them away from Him.

Every day we have the opportunity to write a fresh, new page in our personal legacy—our personal history book. If you haven't written the right kind of legacy in the past, you can start to write a new legacy today—a legacy that will make a difference in someone else's life!

PART I

————◈————

BUILDING YOUR LEGACY

Consecration and Commitment

Chapter 1

---ↀ---

TAKE INVENTORY
OF YOUR LIFE

Every year many people set aside a special time, usually around the first of the year, to take inventory of their personal lives. First, they carefully examine all the projects from last year's to-do list that they didn't finish. Then they formulate their New Year's resolutions for the coming year. They're saying, in essence, *It's a new day and a new year. I'm going to do some new things!*

Taking inventory is a powerful way to help us get a fresh, new start in life. But in my own experience, there have been other times besides the beginning of the year when I've asked the Lord to help me take inventory. For example, I've taken inventory of my life when my prayers don't seem to be answered or when things are just not working right for me.

I say, "God, this is Your promise, and I know Your Word is true. But I haven't received what You promised me. I know the problem is not with You. So what am I doing wrong?"

You see, the promises of God are a partnership. God says, "*If* you'll hearken to My voice and do what I have commanded you to do, *then* you will enjoy My blessings" (see Deut. 28:1–2). The Lord has set down guidelines in His Word. As long as we obey His guidelines, He is obligated to do what He said He would do. But when we're not doing what God has commanded us to do, He doesn't have to hold up His end of the bargain either. That's why it's so important for us to take inventory!

In Psalm 139:23–24, David asked the Lord to help him take inventory of his life. He said, "*Search me [thoroughly], O God, and know my heart! Try me and know my thoughts! And see if there is any wicked or hurtful way in me, and lead me in the way everlasting*" (Amplified).

The Message Bible expresses it this way: "*Investigate my life, O God, find out everything about me; Cross-examine and test me, get a clear picture of what I'm about; See for yourself whether I've done anything wrong—then guide me on the road to eternal life.*"

We all need to take the time on a regular basis to "soul search." We need to say to our Heavenly Father, "Search me, Lord. Take inventory of me. Is there anything I'm doing that You don't want me to do? What do I need to do differently?"

If we want to experience the powerful, victorious Christian life God created us to have, we must allow the Lord to help us take inventory. And when we take our personal inventory, we must make certain that we're living a holy, consecrated life—a life that's set apart, dedicated, and fully devoted to the Lord.

Of course, our Heavenly Father knows that none of us is perfect. We all have faults and imperfections. We all make mistakes. I'm so thankful that we serve a God Who never condemns us. When we slip and make a mistake, all we have to do is ask for His forgiveness. He will forgive us, and He refuses to remember our sins anymore!

A few years ago I decided to take inventory of my life, and God began to deal with me about thinking I was always right. To be perfectly honest, I thought I knew *all* the answers.

One incident really drove this home to me. My best friend, Lanell, and I were shopping for a television set for one of the missionary houses owned by our ministry. After we had selected a TV set, I asked one of the men who worked for us to take the TV over to a certain address.

Lanell quickly piped up, "No, it's not *that* house. That house already has a TV set. It's *this* house." Then she named a different address.

"No," I insisted, "it's *this* house!"

Now Lanell and I are both very competitive and we both think we're always right. So we suddenly found ourselves almost in a knock-down-and-drag-out fight!

Finally, the man who was delivering the TV set decided to call and find out which house actually needed the new TV. A few moments later, he confronted us with the shocking news: "Guess what. Neither of those houses needed a new TV set. It was a completely different house."

Through that experience, I suddenly realized that I am not always right and my way is not always the right way to do things. And I also learned how important it is for me to let God help me take inventory of my life.

The problem with most of us is that we don't want to admit our own faults and shortcomings. We can readily point out every tiny flaw in our spouse, children, or friends. But it's absolutely vital that we say, "Lord, take inventory of *me*."

Besides, when we focus on other people's shortcomings, we're looking through clear glasses. But when others attempt to examine us, we want them to look through rose-colored glasses!

If you're not experiencing the level of victory you desire, I encourage you to let the Lord help you take inventory of your life. Ask yourself, "Am I resentful? Bitter? Jealous? Do I gossip? Stir up strife? Hold grudges?"

Oh, I was a person who always held grudges! I finally had to ask the Lord to give me spiritual amnesia when someone hurt me. That way I could forget all the hurtful things people had said or done to me.

I challenge you today to let the Lord search your heart and help you recognize your own shortcomings. It's so important for you to be honest with yourself. Instead of trying to change everyone around you, be willing to make changes yourself. If you do, it will help you live a more joyful, peaceful life. And I believe you'll discover that the circumstances around you will change as you allow the Lord to change your heart!

Put God First

One of the first questions you should ask yourself when you take inventory of your life is, "Am I putting God first?"

I'm so thankful that I was brought up in a Christian home and learned at an early age to make God the center of my life. My dad, Rev. V.E. Tipton, was a pastor. One of the first scriptures my parents taught me was Matthew 6:33: "*Seek ye first the kingdom of God, and his righteousness; and all these things* [that you need] *shall be added unto you.*"

Even as a little girl, I discovered I had a Friend Who "*sticks closer than a brother*" (Prov. 18:24 NKJV). My Heavenly Father became the most important Person in my life, and I knew I could call upon Him at any moment, day or night.

I thank God that as a child I spent many hours in church with my parents, worshiping God and experiencing the moving of the Spirit. I'm so grateful for the things of the Lord that I learned as we sat around the dinner table while my mother and daddy talked with other ministers.

The spiritual principles that were planted in my heart in those early years have formed a strong foundation for my life. As a result, I developed a habit as a young child of focusing on the things of God and constantly feeding my spirit on the Word and prayer. And that has helped me stay consecrated and dedicated to the Lord throughout my life.

Now I don't want you to think that you have to be involved in some type of spiritual activity 24 hours a day, seven days a week, to be fully consecrated to the Lord. God does not want you to be "so heavenly minded that you're no earthly good."

When it's time to go to work, you need to give your full attention to your job. It's important to give the people you work for an honest day's work. But your job should not prevent you from feeding your spirit the things it needs to grow and prosper.

I also believe God desires for us to have recreational activities we enjoy—perhaps some type of sports event, traveling, or other hobbies. But He does not want those things to be the driving force of our lives. He doesn't want anything to be more important to us than our time with our Heavenly Father!

If you're not experiencing the victory you desire, I encourage you to check up on what you're seeking. Are you seeking the things of this world? Are you seeking money, fame, social position, or professional success? Or are you seeking God first? As you seek first the Kingdom of God and put Him first in your life, everything else will fall into place.

Renew Your Mind

When we ask the Lord to help us take inventory of our lives, one of the most important areas we need to check is that of renewing our minds to the Word of God. In Romans 12:2, the Apostle Paul gives us these powerful instructions: "*And do not be conformed to this world, but be transformed by the renewing of your mind . . .*" (NKJV).

You might wonder, "But I thought my mind *was* renewed when I accepted Jesus Christ as my Lord and Savior." No, when you gave your heart to the Lord, your spirit was instantly made brand-new. You became a new creation in Christ (2 Cor. 5:17). But your flesh was still flesh. You still had the same body to deal with that you had before you were born again. And your mind still had to be renewed through the Word of God.

You still woke up in the morning the same way you did before. You took a shower, brushed your teeth, and combed your hair the same way. And you still had the same temptations to deal with that you had before you became a Christian.

That's why Paul also said in First Corinthians 9:27, "*But I keep under my body, and bring it into subjection: lest that by any means, when I have preached to others, I myself should be a castaway.*" The *Contemporary English Version* puts it this way: "*I keep my body under control and make it my slave, so I won't lose out after telling the good news to others.*"

Let me share a little secret with you today. We all have a carnal nature to deal with, and we will have to deal with that nature until our body is in the grave. The devil has a willing ally in our flesh, and that's what he uses to get us off track. That's one of the reasons why it's so important for us to renew our minds to the Word of God.

How do we renew our minds? By continually feeding our spirits on God's Word. For example, if we're dealing with a certain area of weakness, we can find scriptures to meditate on that will strengthen us in that area. Not only will that help us renew our minds, but when temptation comes, we can focus our faith on what God's Word says about the problem instead of focusing on the problem itself.

Something else we can do to help us deal with our carnal nature is to walk in the Spirit. Galatians 5:16 says that if we walk in the Spirit, we will not fulfill the lust of the flesh. What does it mean to walk in the Spirit? Romans 8:5–6 tells us, *"For those who live according to the flesh set their minds on the things of the flesh, but those who live according to the Spirit, the things of the Spirit. For to be carnally* [or fleshly] *minded is death, but to be spiritually minded is life and peace"* (NKJV).

Notice that these two verses are talking about where we focus our thoughts. Are we focused on the things of the flesh—the things of this world and of our carnal nature? Or is our attention focused on the things of the Spirit—God's Word, prayer, church attendance, and worshipping the Lord?

Stay Surrounded by the Word

I remember a time in my life when I was having trouble finding any peace. I was fighting such a strong spiritual battle that I finally realized I needed to be surrounded by the Word of God 24 hours a day.

Of course, we can't read the Bible 24 hours a day. And we can't spend 24 hours a day on our knees in prayer. We live in a natural world and we have to take care of natural things. No matter what kind of spiritual battle we're facing, we still have to function in life.

Finally, God showed me something I could do to help me keep my mind focused on His Word. I began to play edifying, Spirit-filled worship music in our home, 24 hours a day. Not only did this help build up my spirit and renew my mind, but it also helped keep my spirit at peace.

Before I started playing that music, I was so troubled by all kinds of worrisome thoughts that I couldn't sleep at night.

As I began to play Word songs and songs that talked about the Name of Jesus and the power of His blood, suddenly peace came. And I was able to sleep.

Today our house is filled with Christian music around the clock, seven days a week. I want all of our surroundings to be continually filled with the presence of God. It's important to me for our home to be permeated with God's Word, because I know that His Word is going to build us up spiritually and help us keep our minds renewed.

Why is that so important to me? Because I'm just as human as you are. I have to keep my flesh under just as you do. We all have to keep our bodies under control and bring our minds into subjection to the Word. Really, the battle between the mind and the Spirit is often what gives us the most trouble in life. And continually feeding on God's Word can help us win that battle every time!

Of course, nothing can replace our personal study time in the Word. I have a study Bible that helps me read through the Bible at least once each year.

When you study God's Word, make sure that it's soaking into your spirit. If there are things you don't understand, ask the Lord to illuminate His Word for you. There's nothing more precious than receiving the Word of God!

Proverbs 4:22 says that God's Word is life and health to all our flesh. And Ephesians 5:25–26 tells us that the Lord sanctifies and cleanses us *"with the washing of water by the word."* If we want to enjoy the abundant life God has planned for us, we must keep ourselves surrounded with His Word!

'Resist the Devil'

Another important area we need to check when we take inventory of our lives is that of resisting the devil. James 4:7 tells us, *"Resist the devil, and he will flee from you."* And Hebrews 12:1 says, *". . . let us throw off everything that hinders and the sin that so easily entangles, and let us run with perseverance the race marked out for us"* (NIV). In other words, we must refuse to give in to the temptations that come our way. We have to make a conscious effort to resist them.

One of the most effective things we can do to keep from slipping into sin is not to place ourselves in a compromising position in the first place. Most of us know exactly what our weaknesses are. As much as possible, we need to avoid putting ourselves in a position where we can be tempted to sin.

For example, one of my weaknesses is shopping the sales. To be perfectly honest, I love to go shopping in general, and I know I'm weak in that area.

Many years ago my husband and I were endeavoring to get out of debt. Because I realized that shopping was one of my weaknesses, I decided not to go shopping (except for necessities) for two whole years! In fact, my husband, Ken, and I both agreed to do that. We didn't want to let ourselves be tempted in that area. We were successful in getting out of debt because we avoided placing ourselves in a position to be tempted.

If we truly want to resist temptation, we must remember that the more we feed our spirits on the things of the Lord, the less of a grip temptation will have on us. On the other hand, if we spend too much time doing things that don't feed our spirits, it can weaken our ability to resist temptation.

Let me give you an example of what I'm talking about here. A few years ago I decided to make a CD of some of the beautiful love songs of the '50s and '60s. I wanted to rekindle the memories of my teenage years.

But after I had played that CD for only one day, I was pricked in my spirit that I should not keep listening to those songs. There wasn't anything wrong with those particular songs. They were not ungodly. But they weren't building up my spirit or filling my heart with the Word of God.

It's so important for us to be sensitive to the Lord about *anything* that can hinder our spirituality. It may be something different for you than it was for me. But we all need to stay built up in the Spirit and the Word. Why? Because the temptations of life come to all of us, and the stronger our spirits are, the easier it will be for us to resist those temptations.

Signs and Wonders

When we renew our minds to the Word of God and allow the Holy Spirit to help us resist the devil and control our flesh, then wonderful, miraculous things can happen. In other words, when we consecrate ourselves to the Lord, He can perform His signs and wonders for us.

That's what happened in Joshua chapter 3 when Joshua told the people, "... *Consecrate yourselves, for tomorrow the Lord will do amazing things among you*" (v. 5 NIV). After they had consecrated themselves, God divided the waters of the Jordan River when it was at flood stage. The children of Israel walked across on dry ground!

God wants to do some wondrous things in our lives today. To see those signs, wonders, and miracles, we must be more consecrated and more committed than we've ever been. We must allow God to sanctify us—to purify us. And we must stir ourselves up so we will have a deeper hunger for the things of the Lord than we've ever experienced.

We desperately need to be sanctified—to be purified in this hour. The attitude that has become so prevalent in many Christian circles is, "I'd rather be forgiven than ask for God's permission." Yes, God is a merciful Father. He's a loving and forgiving God. I'm so thankful He's given us provision whereby we can call upon His grace and mercy. But I don't want to lean too heavily on God's grace and mercy. Why? Because He's also a God of judgment.

We don't hear much about the judgment of God in this day. But if we don't judge ourselves, that judgment will come. We can't keep pushing the button to the limit without God judging us!

Why am I warning you about these things? Because the enemy is working overtime to try to trip us up in these areas. We have to stay on guard against the devil because he wants to knock us out of the race if he can. He wants to keep us from having the abundant life Jesus Christ came to provide for us.

That's why we must learn to consecrate and dedicate ourselves to the Lord and draw closer to Him. Second Timothy 2:19 says, ". . . '*The Lord knows those who are really His,*' and *'A person who calls himself a Christian should not be doing things that are wrong'*" (TLB).

The enemy knows his time is short, and he's constantly trying to turn our eyes toward the superficial things of this life—what the Bible calls the things made of wood and clay—so we won't focus on the eternal things, the things made of purest gold. (See 2 Tim. 2:20–21 TLB.) The bottom line is, Satan wants to get our eyes off the goal that God has set before us.

What is that goal? To be a willing vessel, wholly dedicated and consecrated to the Lord.

If we want to see God's plan unfold in this hour, we're going to have to do what the older saints referred to as "crucifying the flesh." What does that mean? It means we must deny our earthly, fleshly desires and say yes to the Father. We must say yes to His Word. We're going to have to say to the Lord, "God, I will be a willing vessel, a clean vessel, to be used for Your service."

I encourage you to let that be your heart's cry, not only today, but every day. And I challenge you to pray this prayer of consecration from your heart:

Heavenly Father, You have made me and I am Yours. I consecrate myself to You. I dedicate my life—my whole mind, soul, spirit, and body—to serving You.

I will keep my body under control. I choose to resist the devil, and he will flee from me. I will be sensitive to Your things and keen to hear Your voice. I will renew my mind to Your Word, and I make up my mind this day that I am going to draw closer to You.

I will walk in faith. I will walk in peace. I will walk with You, O Lord, all the days and nights of my life! My heart and soul cry out for You—my Strength, my Help, and my Redeemer. Amen.

Chapter 2

NEVER SAY 'NEVER'

If you want to enjoy the victorious life God desires for you to have, you must never let the words "I will *never* do that" come out of your mouth.

"I'll *never* go back to my hometown."

"I'll *never* be a missionary."

"I'll *never* marry a minister of the Gospel."

Somehow—I don't know why—it seems that our "nevers" often become the very thing God calls us to do!

When I was a college student, I was a member of a singing group, and we traveled all the time. I detested traveling, so I told my roommate, "I will *never* marry an evangelist because I hate to travel."

Can you guess what my husband's occupation was when we first married? He was an evangelist! I learned the hard way what it means to "eat your 'nevers.'"

What If Jesus Had Said, 'Never'?

Have you ever thought about what would have happened if Jesus Christ had said, "Never!" when the Father asked Him to die on the cross? What if He had not been willing to make the ultimate sacrifice and lay down His life so we could have life more abundantly? Sometimes we take what He did for granted. But He could have told the Father, "This is just too difficult. I can't do it."

What would have happened to us—to mankind—if Jesus had not been willing to sacrifice His life?

Making that kind of ultimate commitment had to be incredibly difficult for our Lord. The Bible records that He said, "... *If it be possible, let this cup pass from me* ..." (Matt. 26:39). He said it not once, but *three* times!

Now that's an inspiration to me. If the perfect, ultimate One found it hard to submit to God's plan, it's no wonder you and I sometimes have difficulty in that area! Following the plan of God for our lives is not always easy. It takes commitment. It takes surrender. It takes a heartfelt determination to follow the Lord.

But what did Jesus say next? "'... *Nevertheless, not as I will, but as You will'*" (v. 39 NKJV). Jesus always submitted Himself to the will of the Father.

Throughout His earthly ministry, the Lord Jesus Christ continually prayed that the will of the Father would be accomplished on this earth. Why do we need to pray that prayer also? Because our flesh is always warring against the will of God. And we have to remind ourselves constantly to stay committed to His will.

The Altar Is a Sacred Place

I remember as a child how the older saints would gather around the altar after every service to seek the Lord. There was a song we sang so many times—"I Surrender All." The first line of that beautiful old hymn says, "All to Jesus I surrender; All to Him I freely give." We were encouraged not only to bring our requests to the altar but to commit our wills to the Lord each time we came.

The altar was a sacred place. It was a place of consecration. It was a place of dedication and commitment. And I believe there are times when we still need to make a connection with the Lord that we can only make when we "go to the altar."

Of course, we've taken the literal, physical altars out of many of our churches today. But we can still have a symbolic altar when we gather at the front of the church and pray. And we can also have a symbolic altar when we simply kneel and pray in our own homes.

In the season we're living in, instead of bringing our "all" to the altar, it seems that many people just want to hear the Word, believe the Word, confess the Word, and receive from the Word. If we're not careful, this process becomes simply a man-made formula. It becomes head knowledge instead of heart knowledge. And that may be one of the reasons why we're not receiving from the Lord.

We're trying to operate a formula that we don't believe in. We're just mimicking what someone else has done. And in so many cases, we're ignoring commitment and consecration. Actually, in today's world, *commitment* is a word we rarely even use!

It seems that people today don't want to commit to anything. They don't want to commit to marriage. They would rather just live together. So often, people don't want to RSVP to a party invitation. They think, *I don't want to make this commitment right now because I may not want to go to this party.* So they don't even bother to reply.

In some cases, I've heard people refer to commitment as bondage. But let me tell you—it's not!

What does the word *commit* mean? It means to give over. It conveys the idea of entrusting, obligating, and binding. I like one of the definitions I found in *Webster's Dictionary*—"to put into a place for safekeeping." We are to commit our whole body, soul, and spirit to the Lord for safekeeping. Really, commitment is saying to God, "I'm committed to Your will, regardless of the cost."

Sometimes commitment can be frightening. When you commit to something or someone else, you lose control to a certain degree. As a supervisor, when I commit a certain responsibility to someone who works for me, I lose some of my control over that project. And that can be hard to deal with sometimes.

David was called a man after God's own heart. Why? Because of his commitment. Acts 13:22 says that God testified of David, "'. . . I have found David son of Jesse a man after my own heart; he will do everything I want him to do'" (NIV). That's real commitment! And Psalm 37:5 says, "*Commit thy way unto the Lord; trust also in him; and he shall bring it to pass.*" When we commit our way to the Lord and trust in Him, who is going to bring His plan to pass? *He is!*

So many times, though, something else happens: instead of committing our way to the Lord and trusting Him to bring it to pass, *we* try to make things happen in our own strength. But the Lord is saying to us, "Trust in Me. Lean on My everlasting arms. Watch and see the wonderful way I bring My plan to pass!"

Stages of Commitment

Did you know that there are several different stages of commitment? Sometimes we think we're one hundred percent committed to God's will, but we really aren't.

As a young girl, I was always sensitive to the things of God and careful to try to follow His will. When I prayed a prayer of commitment, I would say something like this: "Lord, I love You so much, and I want to do what You want me to do. I want to go where You want me to go." I thought I was being so noble when I said those words. But I've discovered that words are cheap. The real question is, do we actually mean what we say?

Then came that fateful day when the Lord asked me to do something I did not want to do. He asked me to go where I did not want to go—to Oklahoma!

"But, Lord," I argued, "I don't want to move. I like living in Dallas!" You see, I came from a very large city, a place where you could always find a good restaurant or some type of shop or establishment open at any hour of the day or night. Your choices were virtually unlimited in Dallas.

But Tulsa, Oklahoma, is a small town by comparison. When God asked us to move to Tulsa, I suddenly discovered I wasn't as committed to doing God's will as I thought I was. In reality, I was only committed to doing what *I* wanted to do.

I finally did make a commitment to follow the Lord's plan and move to Tulsa. But I did it more out of fear than anything else. I was absolutely terrified of being out of the will of God!

You talk about a dark day in my life. When we left Texas to move to Oklahoma, I felt like all of my worst nightmares were being fulfilled. But if we hadn't made that move in obedience to the Lord, we would not have been in position for Him to bless us the way He has over the years.

If you feel as if you're stalled in a holding pattern and you can't seem to reach the next level of God's plan, perhaps you're not fully committed to doing what the Lord has asked you to do right now. He probably won't take you to the next level until you're 100 percent committed to His plan *today*!

As you commit yourself wholly to the Lord and say, "God, if this is what You want me to do for the rest of my life, I'll do it with all of my heart," then you're in the place where God can really use you. And you're also in position for Him to take you to a higher level in His plan!

Don't Be Tempted by Satan's Devices

When you make a strong commitment to the Lord, the enemy will always tempt you to veer away from your commitment. He will come at you where you're the weakest and most vulnerable. But don't be tempted by Satan's devices!

Do you remember the story in the Book of Daniel about the three Hebrew children who refused to bow down to King Nebuchadnezzar's golden image? When the king threatened them with being thrown into his burning, fiery furnace, they replied, "'. . . *our God whom we serve is able to deliver us. . . . But if not, let it be known to you, O king, that we do not serve your gods, nor will we worship the gold image which you have set up*'" (Dan. 3:17–18 NKJV).

Some people call that a statement of unbelief, but I believe it was a statement of the Hebrews' commitment to the Lord. They knew He *could* deliver them, but their commitment was, "Even if He *doesn't*, we're not going to bow down to other gods." And that has to be our commitment today.

What Are Your Ears Tuned To?

If we want to be fully committed to God's will, we need to hear from the Lord for ourselves instead of depending on someone else to hear from God for us. When we actually hear from the Lord personally, it will help us maintain our commitment, even when the enemy is hurling his fiery darts at us!

Let me ask you a thought-provoking question today. Whose instructions are you hearing for your life—God's? Or someone else's? Are you being distracted by the voices of those around you, or even by the voice of the enemy? Are you being distracted by the voice of circumstances? It's so easy to be distracted by all the voices clamoring for our attention.

A few years ago Ken and I were attending the Christian Booksellers Convention, and we had taken a bus from the hotel to the meeting. At every stop, the bus driver called out the name of the street we were crossing. We were supposed to get off at California Street, but there was so much commotion on the bus that we became distracted. Guess what? We missed our stop and had to walk an extra block to get to the convention.

So many times the Holy Spirit is trying to give us instructions. He's trying to give us a nudge. He's saying, "Don't do that. Don't go that way. Go this way." But we don't always understand what He's saying to us.

I've heard my late father-in-law, Kenneth E. Hagin, talk about times when he was ready to leave on a trip and something on the inside—the Holy Ghost—would nudge him, telling him, "Don't leave yet."

I remember him describing one particular time when God warned him to wait before starting on a trip. He obeyed, and later he came upon a horrible traffic accident. If he had left when he had originally planned, he would have been right in the middle of that accident!

It's so easy to get distracted from the plan and purpose God has for your life. But don't let distractions keep you from fulfilling His vision for you.

When the distractions of life come your way, you can tell the devil, "I am on a mission for God, and I am not going to stop now." The enemy will try his best to get you off course and distract you from your commitment. But when he knocks on the door, don't even look through the peephole. Just boldly declare, "Satan, I don't have time for you and your devices!"

Commit Your Way to the Lord

Throughout your life, you will face many crossroads. You will have many opportunities to decide whether to follow your own desires or the will of the Father. Will you put your faith and trust in the Lord or will you "lean to your own understanding" (Prov. 3:5–6)?

One of the worst things that could ever happen to us would be if we stood before the Lord at the end of our lives and He declared, "Halfway well done, thou halfway good and faithful servant," because we only committed to Him halfway! But there's a peace that passes all human understanding that comes only when we're fully committed to Him.

I challenge you today to commit your whole way to the Lord. Walk boldly in His strength and power. And remember, when you're committed to the Father, He will be committed to you.

When temptation comes, when distresses come, and when obstacles come, stay faithful and committed to the Lord. Stay full of the Word and the Spirit. And stay on your knees in prayer. If you do, your life will be a great success for God!

I encourage you to pray this prayer of commitment from your heart:

O Father, not *my will, but Thy will be done. I commit my all to You. I submit to You to lead me and guide me—to direct my steps. It's my desire to walk in Your perfect will. I pray that You will speak to me clearly. And I thank You for giving me Your wisdom to know the right path to take and the right direction to go in.*

I will listen to Your voice. I will not be distracted by the other voices around me. I will march forward in Your ways and lift Your banner high. I will accomplish Your mission and fulfill Your purpose for my life. In the mighty Name of Jesus, I commit my whole being—my all—100 percent to You! Amen.

Chapter 3

IT'S TIME TO GET BACK TO OUR FIRST LOVE

The world today is spinning at such a frantic pace that it's easy to drift away from our first love for the Lord. It's easy to be distracted by other things. But I believe God is calling His people back to our first love.

If we want to experience the victory God intends for us to have, we must have an intimate relationship with our Heavenly Father. We must ask ourselves, "Is my love for the Lord growing stronger every day?" It should be! Our love for God should grow stronger every day just as love for a spouse should always grow stronger and more precious.

When I was first married, I truly loved my husband. But that was only the beginning of love. I really didn't know what love was at the time. The love I felt for my husband then was just a smidgen of the love I feel for him now.

We've been married since 1965, and we love each other more today than we did on the day when we said, "Till death do us part." Our love has grown stronger over the years, and our love for the Lord Jesus Christ should be the same way!

One of the most powerful ways I know to deepen our love for the Lord is to delight ourselves in God and His Word.

Psalm 37:4 says, "*Delight yourself in the Lord and he will give you the desires of your heart*" (NIV).

Psalm 1:1–3 also tells us, "*Blessed is the man that walketh not in the counsel of the ungodly, nor standeth in the way of sinners, nor sitteth in the seat of the scornful. BUT HIS DELIGHT is in the law of the Lord* [God's Word]; *and in his law doth he meditate day and night. And . . . whatsoever he doeth shall prosper.*"

I learned at an early age that if I delighted in the Lord and in His Word, He would be pleased with me and whatever I did would prosper. Even as a young child, I loved to commune with my Heavenly Father. I don't remember a time in my life when I wasn't praying or seeking the Lord.

At the age of 4, I began to go to the altar and pray with the adults during our church services. Such a deep hunger for God was stirred up in me during those times! Why? Because I could sense the Presence of my Heavenly Father, and that made me want even more of Him!

In these stressful and challenging times, we need to have a burning desire for more of God. Why is that so important? Because a strong relationship with the Lord is the only thing that's going to get us through in these last days. But the world today is so chaotic that we sometimes forget about delighting in the Lord.

Distracted by Doing Good

Satan is very subtle and crafty. If he can't get us off track by luring us into sin, he'll do his best to dominate our time by getting us to do good deeds. He'll try to keep us from having any time to spend in the Word or prayer—in developing our relationship with our Heavenly Father.

There's a passage in Luke chapter 10 that describes what I'm talking about here.

LUKE 10:38-42

38 Now it came to pass, as they went, that he [Jesus] entered into a certain village: and a certain woman named Martha received him into her house.

39 And she had a sister called Mary, which also sat at Jesus' feet, and heard his word.

40 But Martha was cumbered about much serving, and came to him, and said, Lord, dost thou not care that my sister hath left me to serve alone? bid her therefore that she help me.

41 And Jesus answered and said unto her, Martha, Martha, thou art careful and troubled about many things:

42 But one thing is needful: and Mary hath chosen that good part, which shall not be taken away from her.

Mary had chosen the good part! That really strikes home with me. So many times in dealing with the nitty-gritty details of life, I get trapped in "the Martha syndrome." I become extremely busy taking care of all the natural things. We certainly need to take care of the natural things—yet in the midst of doing those things, we cannot forget about communing with our Heavenly Father.

Of course, while I'm busy being "Martha," I always feel that the "Marys" aren't doing anything at all. I feel as if I'm the one who is doing all the work while the "Marys" are just enjoying themselves with the Lord. Meanwhile, the enemy is doing his best to keep me occupied doing busywork for God!

But do you know what? While we Marthas are doing all the work, we may suddenly find our lives in a state of havoc because we've neglected the most important thing—delighting ourselves in the Lord. We've neglected to sit at Jesus' feet.

Then we try to triple up on doing the Mary part—"Oh, we love You, Lord! We praise You, Father!" And God in His mercy always comes through for us. But how much better would it be if we learned how to balance the Mary role with the Martha role—if we learned to spend more of our time basking in the presence of our Father?

It's so important not to let even *good* things rob us of our time with our Heavenly Father. We need to set aside time regularly to study the Word, be in the presence of the Lord, worship Him, and pray.

And remember, everyone is different. You don't have to rise at 5 o'clock in the morning to pray and read the Word. If that's what you like to do, that's wonderful.

If I tried to pray at 5 o'clock in the morning, I would sleep more than I would pray. If I tried to read the Bible at 5 o'clock in the morning, I'd read one verse and then I'd fall fast asleep. I'm not going to be very fruitful in worshipping the Lord if I'm trying to wake up my flesh!

I encourage you to find a time to fellowship with the Lord that works best for you. But make sure that you *do* spend time communing with Him. It's so important for you to read the Word and develop your relationship with your Heavenly Father. Those are the things that will help you keep your love for God fresh and strong!

Hungering and Thirsting for the Lord

Matthew 5:6 says, *"Blessed are they which do hunger and thirst after righteousness: for they shall be filled."* And the psalmist expressed his hunger for the Lord in Psalm 42:1–2 when he said, *"As the deer pants for water, so I long for you, O God. I thirst for God, the living God. Where can I find him to come and stand before him?"* (TLB).

Our Heavenly Father desires so much for us to hunger and thirst for the things of God. Spiritual things should never become stale or commonplace to us.

I've been saved for over 60 years, but I'm just as excited about the things of God today as I was 60 years ago. My heart is just as tender to the Lord now as it was then. And it's absolutely vital that we keep that excitement and expectation stirring in us.

In the area of "natural" hunger, Mexican food is one of my favorites. I have an appetite for that type of food fairly often. In fact, I could eat Mexican food several times a week if my diet would allow it.

But Mexican food can be extremely filling. After I've enjoyed a good Mexican meal, it may be a couple of days before I'm hungry for that type of food again.

That's not the way it should be concerning our hunger for the Word and the things of the Spirit. God wants us to hunger and thirst continually for the things of the Lord.

I grew up in the Pentecostal movement, and I remember how enthusiastic we were when we first learned how to use our faith and believe God. While I was a student in Bible school, I remember one professor saying that when the school started, they would have to pray and ask God to provide the food they needed for the students each day. In the morning they would ask the Lord for food, and by noon God would provide food for them. What an exciting time that must have been in their faith walk with the Lord!

When the Pentecostal movement began, people were really on fire for God. There was such an urgency about the things of the Lord and a powerful moving of the Spirit.

But over time, the Pentecostals seemed to lose their zeal and excitement for spiritual things. They became settled in their ways. The things of God became "business as usual." You see, they thought they were the only ones who could enjoy the power of the Holy Spirit. In some cases, they even began to take the moving of the Spirit for granted.

Do you know what? God will not allow His power to be relegated to a box! Suddenly the Lord began to move among the denominational churches. Out of the complacency of the Pentecostals came the fire of the Charismatic movement!

All at once, the denominations became stirred up about the Lord. Their hearts were hungry for more of God, and God showed himself mightily in their midst.

When the Charismatic movement began, people were so thrilled by the things of the Lord because they were experiencing the whole Gospel and the reality of the Word for the first time. Believers from all denominations were being filled with the Holy Spirit and proudly proclaiming it!

The Holy Ghost came out of the box the Pentecostals had tried to put Him in, and the fire of the Spirit began spreading all over the earth. A tremendous move of God's power was shaking our world, and my husband and I jumped right into the middle of it!

Then the Pentecostals began to say, "Just give the Charismatics a few years and they'll settle down." When I heard that, I said to myself, *I am not going to lose my excitement for the Lord! I am not going to lose my desire to hear more of God's Word and be inspired by it. In Jesus' Name, I refuse to settle down!*

Unfortunately, some of the predictions that were made about the Charismatic movement have already come to pass. Some Charismatics are not hungering and thirsting after God as they once were. They've settled down. The fire has grown cold.

Even those in the Word of Faith movement are not hungry to hear about faith like they were in the 1980s. Not only that, but they're not exercising the Word of God. They're not practicing what they've heard. We all need to stir ourselves up about the things of God, especially since we have such a great work to do in these last days!

I believe we're at a crossroads in the Charismatic and Word of Faith movement. Are we going on with God? Are we going to flow with the next great wave of revival? Are we going to boldly proclaim the power and anointing of the Lord? Or are we going to sit on the sidelines of life and merely watch? Are we going to miss out on the moving of the Spirit?

I tell you, this is burning on the inside of me! I believe there should be such a hunger for God in this hour that every church should be full and running over. It seems that there's been a lull in the enthusiasm of the church world over the past few years. People haven't been as hungry for the things of God as they once were. But I sense in my spirit a fresh, new hunger for the Lord rising up in people's hearts!

We must shake ourselves out of our complacency. It's time that we draw closer to God than ever before. He has some specific assignments for us in these last days, and the only way we're going to be able to clearly understand those assignments is to develop a closer relationship with our Heavenly Father.

As we earnestly open our hearts to the Lord, He will make Himself so real and so dear to us. We'll experience divine visitations and a new wave of His power—a new outpouring of the Spirit!

I believe the Lord wants us to stir ourselves up in this hour. He wants us to stir up an excitement in our hearts for a mighty move of God. When we who are His people begin to stir ourselves up, we'll see those out there in the world who don't know the Lord become stirred up too. And the convicting power of the Holy Ghost will cause the lost to come streaming in!

Chapter 4

THE FEAR OF THE LORD

The fear of the Lord is a powerful spiritual force. It can keep us on the right path in life, and it can also keep us out of trouble. The fear of the Lord is so important for our well-being, and yet it seems to be so lacking in the church world today.

What is the fear of the Lord? It's a reverence for God and the things of the Lord. It's a deep respect for the holiness of God and a godly fear of displeasing our Heavenly Father.

The fear of the Lord is *not* the kind of fear that some have experienced because they believe God is just waiting to punish them when they make a mistake. The true fear of the Lord should be motivated by our love for our Heavenly Father. We love God so much and we're so deeply grateful for everything He's done for us that we desperately want to please Him and make Him proud of us. And we don't want to do anything that would hurt or displease our Father.

I thank God that the fear of the Lord was instilled in me from the time I was a little child. When I was growing up, we were taught to have a godly reverence for the things of God. When the gifts of the Spirit were in operation during a church service, the minute someone began to utter a tongue, an interpretation, or a prophecy, we all bowed our heads and were quiet and reverent.

We were also taught that you're supposed to be quiet when you come to the house of God, that you should show reverence for His house. Why? Because the house of God is sacred. It's a holy place. And I believe we would experience more of God's power and His presence if we began to reverence Him more and get back to that godly fear of the Lord!

God Is Always With You

When I was a little girl my daddy told me, "Honey, God is with you every moment of the day. You may hide something from your dad, but you're never going to hide it from the Lord." So I developed the guideline early in life: if God were here with me—and even as a child I knew that He was always with me—would I be doing what I'm doing right now?

Really, we would all be more careful about our words and actions if we had the attitude that our Heavenly Father is with us at all times and He sees and hears everything we do and say. We'd be so much more careful about what we say and where we go.

When you think about the Lord seeing everything you do, it might cause you to wonder if He would be pleased with what you've been doing today. When you think about the Lord hearing everything you say, it might make you examine the words that come out of your mouth when you get upset. Does God hear you curse His Name or bless His Name?

I admonish you to guard yourself continually. Always keep in mind that the Lord is looking down upon you. It's not worth it to engage in activities that would be displeasing to Him. The cost is too great, and it could damage your relationship with your Heavenly Father.

God's Keeping Power

I am so thankful that I have a testimony of the way God has kept me through the years instead of a testimony of all the things He's had to deliver me from. The main reason for this is that I've always had a deep, reverential fear of the Lord.

I'm not bragging on myself when I make that statement. I'm bragging on God and I'm also bragging on my godly parents who were faithful to train me in the things of the Lord. The principles they taught me are still alive in my heart today. Those principles have kept me all of these years, even through the most treacherous storms of life.

I remember how strongly I was influenced by the fear of the Lord growing up, even as a small child. My first day of school was a traumatic experience for me because I had never been away from my mother. I was so nervous as I ate my lunch that day that I forgot to say the blessing over my food.

Up until that moment, I had *never* eaten a meal without saying grace. I didn't even know you could eat a meal without saying the blessing. That's just something my family had always done.

When I went home from school that afternoon, all of a sudden I realized I had not blessed my lunch that day. I was so mortified that I actually thought I had committed the unpardonable sin!

Now you may be thinking, *Lynette, that's a little over-board, isn't it?*

Perhaps it was, but my conscience was so tender to the Lord that it pricked me sharply. I was brokenhearted that I had forgotten to bless my food because that's how I had been trained by my parents.

It's so important for us to maintain a conscience that's tender to the Lord. We must not override our conscience, lest it becomes seared, as the Bible talks about in First Timothy 4:2.

Keep Your Conscience Tender!

Every day I make an effort to keep my conscience tender to the Lord. I want it to prick me immediately if I stray from the things God desires for me to do. Why? Because it's the convicting power of God that leads me, guides me, and directs me throughout my life.

I remember when I was growing up how the preachers would deliver those fiery sermons about Heaven and hell and the consequences of sin. They described in vivid detail how two would be in the field when the Lord returns. One was going to be taken and the other left behind. By the time they had finished preaching, the whole congregation was ready to flock to the altar and repent. We knew we were already right with the Lord, but we wanted to get right with Him again, just to be on the safe side!

I don't see people crowding the altars today the way we used to when I was a child. I don't sense the fear of the Lord in our services the way I did during my early years. In some cases, I believe people's consciences have become seared, which may be one of the reasons why their prayers aren't being answered.

As you're reading my words today, you may have realized that your conscience has become seared. You may be so hardened in certain areas that it doesn't even bother you when you do something wrong. Let me tell you, you're living on dangerous ground! God has placed your conscience within you as a guideline. And if you're not sensitive to your conscience, as well as to the leading of the Holy Spirit, you're going to miss out!

The Lord is constantly trying to lead you and guide you. If you want to experience all the good things He has prepared for you, you must keep your heart tender to Him.

'*Go and Sin No More*'

It tears my heart out when I see people who have trampled on their conscience for so long that they don't have any idea how to have a godly, holy fear of their Heavenly Father. But thank God, our conscience can be restored. We can become sensitive to the Holy Spirit again!

There are several things we can do if we want our conscience to become more tender to the Lord. First of all, as we continually obey God's Word, our conscience will become more sensitive and tender to the Holy Spirit. Also, the more time we spend in prayer and communing with our Heavenly Father, the more receptive our spirits are going to be to hearing His voice.

Of course, as I've mentioned previously, God is a God of grace and mercy. When we miss the mark, all we have to do is ask Him to forgive us. But we do need to repent. We need to be truly sorry for the things we've done wrong. And we also need to be deeply grateful for the grace of God that sets us free from our sins.

After we repent, God will lift us up, just as He did the woman in John chapter 8 who was caught in the act of adultery. And Jesus will say to us as He did to her, "... *'Neither do I condemn you ...'*" (v. 11 NKJV). But notice what He said in the rest of that verse—"*'... go and sin no more.'*"

I admonish you today: If you've asked God to forgive you, know that He has forgiven you. But always remember the words of Jesus—go and sin no more!

And be sure to do as Paul said in Galatians 5:1: "*Stand fast therefore in the liberty wherewith Christ hath made us free, and be not entangled again with the yoke of bondage.*" In other words, don't allow the devil to put that yoke of sin back on you!

You may have been delivered from drugs or alcohol. You may have been set free from homosexuality. You may have been trapped in the miry clay in some other area of your life, but now the Lord has delivered you and set you free.

No matter what you've been delivered from, the enemy will always try to make you slip back into sin. But don't let Satan bring those things of the world back into your life. Don't ever entertain those temptations again.

Stay Close to the Savior

There are so many reasons why we should desire to have the fear of the Lord operating in our lives. But the most important reason is that we love our Heavenly Father and want to stay close to Him. Our relationship with Him should be the most dear and precious thing in the world to us. It should be so important that we wouldn't want *anything* to come between us and our Savior. That's the real reason we need to have a godly fear of the Lord.

As we maintain a conscience that's tender toward God, it will strengthen our relationship with our Heavenly Father. And the more we honor and reverence Him, the more we'll experience His presence and His miracle-working power!

Chapter 5

OH, THE LOVE WALK!

In Deuteronomy chapter 28, Moses gave the children of Israel some powerful instructions concerning what they must do if they wanted to receive the blessings of God. He said, *". . . if thou shalt hearken diligently unto the voice of the Lord thy God, to observe and to do all his commandments which I command thee this day, that the Lord thy God will set thee on high above all nations of the earth: And all these blessings shall come on thee, and overtake thee . . ."* (vv. 1–2). Then Moses listed all the wonderful blessings that are available to us as believers.

He declared that we'll be blessed in the city, blessed in the field, and blessed in our storehouses. We'll be blessed coming in and blessed going out. But these blessings are not automatic. In verse 13, Moses repeated his instructions concerning how we can activate God's blessings. The blessings come when we *". . . heed the commandments of the Lord . . . and are watchful to do them"* (Amplified).

What are the commandments God has asked us to do? Throughout the Word of God, we've been given many specific commandments. But in Matthew chapter 22, Jesus said that all the commandments could be summed up in two.

MATTHEW 22:36–40

36 Master, which is the great commandment in the law?

37 Jesus said unto him, Thou shalt love the Lord thy God with all thy heart, and with all thy soul, and with all thy mind.

38 This is the first and great commandment.

39 And the second is like unto it, Thou shalt love thy neighbour as thyself.

40 On these two commandments hang all the law and the prophets.

What was Jesus saying here? If we operate in love, we won't have to try to keep all the other commandments. Why? Because we will already be obeying them. And the Apostle Paul also declared in Galatians 5:14, "*For all the law is fulfilled in one word, even in this: 'You shall love your neighbor as yourself'*" (NKJV).

What does love do? It shows compassion. It forgives and forgets. It keeps itself from guile. Love doesn't say hurtful things. It doesn't gossip. It refuses to judge others.

I have a favorite saying concerning God's command not to judge others: "If you haven't been in someone else's shoes, don't say what you would do if you were in their place. Instead, ask yourself, 'How would I want to be treated if I were that person?'"

It's so important not to judge others. Someone may be going through an extreme crisis. They may be hurting terribly. But instead of putting soothing oil, a healing balm, on those wounds, many times we judge the person and say cutting words. We wrap our self-righteous rags around us as the

Pharisees did and leave no room for people to make a mistake and be forgiven. We Christians are often the worst at killing our own wounded!

Instead, the Church should be a loving place. Christians should be loving people. Let's read how love is described in *The Amplified Bible*:

1 CORINTHIANS 13:4-8 (Amplified)

4 Love endures long and is patient and kind; love never is envious nor boils over with jealousy, is not boastful or vainglorious, does not display itself haughtily.

5 It is not conceited (arrogant and inflated with pride); it is not rude (unmannerly) and does not act unbecomingly. Love (God's love in us) does not insist on its own rights or its own way, for it is not self-seeking; it is not touchy or fretful or resentful; it takes no account of the evil done to it [it pays no attention to a suffered wrong].

6 It does not rejoice at injustice and unrighteousness, but rejoices when right and truth prevail.

7 Love bears up under anything and everything that comes, is ever ready to believe the best of every person, its hopes are fadeless under all circumstances, and it endures everything [without weakening].

8 Love never fails [never fades out or becomes obsolete or comes to an end]. . . .

Oh, the love walk! I believe we've only begun to scratch the surface of the commandment of love!

You see, God wants us to operate in love at all times . . . and with everybody. We have to constantly practice walking in love.

Sometimes we think we're doing such a fine job of practicing our love walk, but then all at once, someone comes along and throws us a curve. They do something awful to us. They insult us or hurt our feelings. Suddenly, we don't want to walk in love anymore.

It hurts when somebody says something ugly about me. And when they criticize me it makes me want to cry. But after I finish crying, I get mad, and I have an overwhelming urge to tell that person off. I want to say to them, "Who do you think you are to judge me?" But God desires for us to operate in love.

My father-in-law was an outstanding example of someone who always walked in love. It didn't matter what anyone said or did to Brother Hagin, he always chose to operate in love.

One of the things that's inspired me to walk in love through the years was hearing my father-in-law say over and over again, "Mark 11:23 and 24 won't work if you don't practice Mark 11:25—if you don't forgive." And he always reminded us of Galatians 5:6, which says, "Faith . . . worketh by love." I knew I needed my faith to work, so I made up my mind to walk in love and forgive!

Did you know that forgiveness is not forgiveness unless you forget about the wrong that was done to you? I looked up the word *forgive* in *Webster's Dictionary*, and one of the definitions is, "to cease to feel resentment against (an offender)."

As I mentioned previously, I've struggled in the past with holding grudges. It was always hard for me to forget the hurtful things that were done to me. So I finally prayed for the

Lord to give me spiritual amnesia when something painful happened.

From that time to this, as soon as I forgive someone, God helps me forget what they've done. If someone else brings those painful things to my remembrance, I think to myself, *Why, I don't even remember that!*

To be perfectly honest, if you don't forgive, you're only hurting yourself. You're not hurting the person you haven't forgiven. Unforgiveness is only going to cause *you* problems. And if you let it fester, a root of bitterness will creep into your heart.

The Apostle Peter must have had a problem with forgiveness because in Matthew 18:21, he asked Jesus, "... *Lord, how oft shall my brother sin against me, and I forgive him? till seven times?*"

In the next verse Jesus replied, "... *I say not unto thee, Until seven times: but, Until seventy times seven.*" That's 490 times! I seriously doubt that anyone is going to offend us 490 times in our lifetime. But if it happens, we must still forgive.

I remember Brother Hagin sometimes using the example of two families in a church he pastored to illustrate the importance of forgiveness. The mother in one of the families said to him, "Brother Hagin, there's something I just don't understand. The so-and-so family lives right only about half the time, but every time they get sick, they pray and immediately get healed. On the other hand, our family has always lived right. We've always walked the straight and narrow path. We've tithed and been faithful to serve the Lord. But when our family gets sick, we pray and we never seem to get healed. I want to know why!"

My father-in-law said to her, "Unless the Lord reveals the exact reason to me, I can't tell you why. But I *can* give you some hints as to what the reason might be."

Then he continued, "I know the such-and-such family (and he named the other family she had mentioned). They're loving, forgiving people. But there are other families who don't love or forgive easily. Your family may fall into that category."

"Oh, yes! We do," this woman exclaimed. "We always hold grudges and we have a terrible time forgiving people."

"That's your answer," Brother Hagin replied. "You need to let go of the hurtful things and forgive. If you don't, you're going to stop the blessings of God from flowing in your life."

The same thing is true for you and me today. If we hold something against someone, it will stop the flow of God's blessings to us. But if we can learn to let those things go, it will release us from the bondage of unforgiveness!

The Pain of Betrayal

One of the deadliest traps the enemy can set for us is to cause us to get offended. Of course, if it's a sinner who offends us, it's not as difficult for us to forgive as it is when we're wounded by another Christian—by someone who is supposed to be practicing love. And what if someone who we thought was our friend hurts us or does us harm?

In Psalm 55:12-14, the psalmist talks about the pain of being betrayed by a friend: *"If an enemy were insulting me, I could endure it; if a foe were raising himself against me, I could hide from him. But it is you, a man like myself, my companion, my close friend, with whom I once enjoyed sweet fellowship as we walked with the throng at the house of God"* (NIV).

Oh, the pain of betrayal! There's nothing worse than being stabbed in the back by a friend. Your best friend may offend you, but don't let offense lodge in your heart. Always take the high road and walk the love path. Don't allow offenses to cause you to stumble!

Many years ago I had a particular friend who hurt me terribly. We had always enjoyed our time together, and I had given a lot of myself in that relationship. But all of a sudden, she turned on me.

I don't cry easily. In fact, about the only time I cry is when I feel overwhelmed or if something hurts me badly. But when this incident happened, I fell apart. I began to cry profusely because I was so devastated by my friend's betrayal.

My dad happened to be at our house at the time, and I poured out my heart to him about the situation. "Daddy," I cried out, "I'm so tired of giving to people and investing in them and being hurt in return. I'm not going to do that anymore. I'm just going to do things for myself, and that way I won't get hurt!"

My dad said to me, "Honey, you wouldn't be happy without investing in people's lives and giving to them. You live to give." And he was right.

Then he told me, "Lynette, why don't you go to First Peter chapter 4 and read verse 8." That verse says, " '. . . *Love will cover a multitude of sins*' " (NKJV). Once again, my dad encouraged me (as he always had) to walk in love. And I challenge you today: Don't allow offenses to trip you up and rob you of your victory. Choose to walk in love!

Refuse to Take On Someone Else's Offense

Do you realize how often we take on someone else's offense? I'll never forget a wonderful, loyal employee who worked for my husband and me in the ministry many years ago. I've never known anyone who had a greater loyalty and commitment to us than this man had. He loved Ken and me with all of his heart.

At the same time, we had another employee who had so much bitterness and animosity toward us that he was constantly saying critical things behind our backs. Every time our loyal employee heard this man say something ugly or hurtful about us, it crushed his spirit.

One day he was talking to me about this situation, and he blurted out, "It irritates and upsets me so much when he talks about you that way!"

I'll never forget as long as I live what I said to that dear man. I called him by his name and told him, "You've got to let this go. We've already forgiven this man. Please let it go."

But he continued, "I can't let it go! It upsets me too much."

I felt such an urgency about the situation that I admonished him again, "You've got to let this go or it's going to kill you."

Little did I know that I was speaking to him prophetically that day. Our wonderful, faithful employee couldn't seem to turn loose of that offense, and he died prematurely of a heart attack. You see, when we hold those negative emotions inside us, it can be extremely damaging to our health.

What does the Bible say we're supposed to do when we're dealing with our enemies, with those who say evil things against us (or against someone we love)? Matthew 5:44 tells us, "... *Love your enemies, bless them that curse you, do good to them that hate you, and pray for them which despitefully use you, and persecute you."*

We're supposed to pray for our enemies. That's something I've always had difficulty doing. In fact, because it's been so difficult for me, the first scripture I read every day when I meditate on God's Word is Matthew 5:44.

Regardless of what anyone may do or say to me or how they may hurt me, I've made a decision that I'm going to obey God's Word and pray for my enemies. Of course, my flesh always wants to rise up. I want to pray for my enemies, all right! But I want to pray, "Lord, please make harm come to them."

I do not want to pray, "God, please bless that person." But on the other hand, I know if I don't keep my attitude right, God can't bless me!

It's Too Hard to Walk in Love

You may feel that it's just too hard for you to walk in love. But I want to share what I do when I need help with my love walk.

If I start to feel short-tempered and out of sorts, or if I begin to get irritated at small things, I first check up on how much time I've been spending in prayer. The more you stay in close relationship with your Heavenly Father, the easier it is to forgive. Why? Because your carnal nature is being put under.

Also, Romans 5:5 tells us that the love of God is shed abroad in our hearts by the Holy Ghost. The more time I spend in prayer, especially praying in the Spirit, the more the love of God fills my heart. And that makes it a whole lot easier for me to walk in love!

I also check up on how much time I've been spending in the Word. The only reason we can walk in love in the first place is because God gives us the strength and self-control to do it. We cannot do it in our own strength. And the two primary ways we can draw strength from the Lord are through His Word and prayer. When we neglect those things, it's easy to get out of sorts and out of fellowship, not only with our fellow man, but also with God.

One of the greatest examples I know of someone Who prayed for His enemies is the Lord Jesus Christ. When He was crucified, so many horrible things were said and done to Him. But He still prayed for those who hurt Him. He said, "*. . . Father, forgive them; for they know not what they* *do*" (Luke 23:34). And that's a good prayer for us to pray when someone hurts us.

You may be feeling awful pain this very moment because of what someone has said or done to you. Maybe they've taken advantage of you. Perhaps they've cheated you in a business deal and you've harbored that hurt in your heart. Or maybe they've said something about you that wasn't true—something extremely hurtful.

If there's anyone you need to forgive, I urge you to pray and forgive them right now. Just say, "Father, I forgive that person and I choose to forget." Then let go of the hurt in your heart.

I made a decision many years ago that I didn't care how badly anyone hurt me. I was going to practice what our Lord Jesus Christ practiced on the cross. I was going to say, "Father, forgive them for they know not what they do." And then I was going to refuse to remember the hurt anymore.

Ephesians 5:2 tells us, "*. . . And walk in love, as Christ also hath loved us, and hath given himself for us an offering and a sacrifice to God for a sweetsmelling savour.*" Did you know that when you walk in love it has a sweet-smelling fragrance before your Heavenly Father—the sweet savor of the love walk? And everywhere you go, people are going to experience the fragrance of the Lord Jesus Christ . . . simply because you've chosen to walk in love!

PART II

FAITH TO CONQUER

Chapter 6

THE FOUR F'S OF SUCCESS

When you read the title of this chapter, you may think that an F doesn't sound too successful. Normally you get an F when you fail a subject in school. But if you want to succeed in your Christian walk, the four F's I'm about to share with you are going to be a tremendous benefit.

Stay FOCUSED

One of the most important things you must do if you want to be successful in life is to stay focused. In this day and age, sometimes it's difficult to do that because we have so many choices.

For example, when we, in the United States, go to the grocery store to buy cereal, we're faced with an abundance of choices. If we travel overseas, we might find only a few brands of cereal. Or we might find one brand of deodorant instead of the variety we have in the U.S. When we have an abundance of choices, it can be easy to get confused in making a selection.

Some years ago, I desperately needed a computer to use in my work. Our son was in charge of buying computers for our ministry, so I said to him, "Son, I want a computer." But six months later, I still didn't have one. So I asked him, "Why haven't you bought me a computer?"

"They're about to come out with several new features," he replied, "and I don't know which computer would be the best for you."

"But Son," I insisted, "I really need a computer now. Please buy me one."

Finally, a whole year had passed and I still didn't have a computer. So I asked my son about it again.

"Mother," he replied, "they're about to come out with some brand-new technology, and the computers that are available right now will be totally obsolete when the new ones come out."

At that point, I became exasperated. "Son!" I exclaimed. "I don't care what's going to come out. I need a computer *now*. Please just buy me a computer!" Sometimes we can get so confused by many choices that we don't make any choice at all!

You will have many opportunities in life to get sidetracked from doing what God has called you to do. I cannot tell you how many times people have asked my husband and me about the programs at RHEMA Bible Church where we are pastors. They've said, "Why don't you have this program or that program in the church?"

It would be so easy for us to say, "Oh, yes. We're going to do that." But guess what? We would become sidetracked from doing what God has called us to do. Even now when we receive ideas or suggestions, we have to go to the Lord and say, "God, is this what You want us to focus on?" It's so important to stay focused on what God has called us to do!

What does *focus* mean? Among its meanings are "a center of interest," "a focal point," and "the center of attention."

If you're not careful, your focus will become "hindsighted." That's what happened to the children of Israel in the wilderness. Moses led them out of Egypt toward the Promised Land, but their focus was all wrong. They kept looking back. Every time something went wrong or they became frightened, they cried out to Moses, "Why didn't you leave us back there in Egypt?"

When troubles and trials befall us, it's so easy to start looking back. It's easy to say, "I should have stayed where I was. Things were so much better before I took this step of faith and landed in the mess I'm in today." But you can't go forward if you're always looking back!

I encourage you today to refuse to look back. Focus on what's ahead. The Apostle Paul said in Philippians 3:13–14, "... *Forgetting those things which are behind, and reaching forth unto those things which are before, I press toward the mark for the prize of the high calling of God in Christ Jesus.*" Paul is saying, "Press on! Press on!" You'll never have the success you desire if you're always looking in the rearview mirror of life!

What is our focus supposed to be? What is our true mission in life? Let's focus on how we can win the lost to the Lord. Jesus said in Mark 16:15, "... *Go ye into all the world, and preach the gospel to every creature.*" Jesus' ever-consuming desire was to reach down and snatch lost souls out of the pit of hell.

We should never lose sight of our greatest mission—to go to a dying world and win the lost to Christ. We have an obligation to tell people everywhere the good news of the Gospel. The Great Commission should be our most important focus in life.

Stay FIXED

God has provided tremendous victory for us through His Word, but if we want to experience that victory, we must keep our hearts fixed on the Lord. It's important for us to be fixed on Jesus not only as our Savior, but also as our Healer, our Provider, and our Rock. And we must always keep our hearts fixed on His Word.

Psalm 112:6–7 says, "*Surely he* [the upright] *shall not be moved for ever: the righteous shall be in everlasting remembrance. He shall not be afraid of evil tidings: his heart is fixed, trusting in the Lord.*"

When you hear some kind of bad report, you need to plant your foot firmly on the Rock—the Lord Jesus Christ— and say, "Devil, my foot is on the Rock and my mind is made up. I put you on notice—I am going to make it!"

When temptation comes your way, you can say, "My foot is on the Rock, and I'm going to stay on that Rock. Satan, you will not lead me astray!"

When sickness comes knocking on your door, just say to the devil, "I put you on notice. My foot is on the Rock. I'm posting my 'No Trespassing' signs. You will not make my body sick!"

When you're struck by financial difficulties, you can declare, "Satan, my foot is on the Rock and I'm fixed on God's

Word. Philippians 4:19 says that my God will supply all of my needs according to His riches in glory by Christ Jesus!"

When discouragement comes, you can proclaim by faith, "Devil, you cannot discourage me because my foot is on the Rock. I can't go under for going over! I will make it through this situation because I can do all things through Jesus Christ (Phil. 4:13)."

Whatever kind of attack comes against you, you can boldly declare, "My heart is fixed on the Word, and the Word says that God will be with me in trouble. Not only will He be with me, but He will also deliver me (Ps. 91:14–15). And He always causes me to triumph in Christ (2 Cor. 2:14)!"

We need to make sure that our anchor is secure, that our foundation is firmly fixed on God's Word. Then when the waves of turmoil, trials, and tribulations come, we can stay steady on the Word of God.

Our hearts and minds should be so fixed on the Lord Jesus Christ that we can say what the Apostle Paul said in Romans chapter 8.

ROMANS 8:35, 37–39

35 Who shall separate us from the love of Christ? shall tribulation, or distress, or persecution, or famine, or nakedness, or peril, or sword? . . .

37 Nay, in all these things we are more than conquerors through him that loved us.

38 For I am persuaded, that neither death, nor life, nor angels, nor principalities, nor powers, nor things present, nor things to come,

39 Nor height, nor depth, nor any other creature, shall be able to separate us from the love of God, which is in Christ Jesus our Lord.

We have to let the devil know that we're going to keep our foot on the Rock, no matter what. Nothing is going to deter us. We must keep our hearts and minds fixed on the Deliverer—the Lord Jesus Christ.

Satan is the oppressor, but Jesus Christ is the Deliverer. Satan will try to get us off track, but he is under our feet.

Remember, you don't have to defeat the devil yourself. Your elder Brother, Jesus, has already defeated him. When your heart and mind are fixed on the Lord, you will not be moved from your position of victory!

Be FAITHFUL

Did you know that you are planting seeds today that will produce a harvest in your life tomorrow? But what kind of seeds are you planting? Are you planting seeds of faithfulness?

Luke 16:10 says, *"He that is faithful in that which is least is faithful also in much. . . ."* And verse 12 goes on to say, *"And if ye have not been faithful in that which is another man's, who shall give you that which is your own?"* In other words, we must be faithful in helping others fulfill their vision before God will help us fulfill our vision.

It's so vital for us to be faithful. Faithfulness is one of the fruit of the Spirit described in Galatians 5:22. And God wants us to be faithful in every area of our lives.

The Lord wants us to be faithful in our church attendance and faithful in listening while the pastor preaches. He also wants us to be faithful at work. He doesn't want us to stay home just because we feel a little under the weather or because we only had three hours of sleep the night before. If we go to work in faith, God will meet us there!

I can't tell you how many times I've gone to work when I was tired or didn't feel well. But God has always rewarded me for being faithful to my employer.

The Lord also wants us to be faithful to our spouses, families, and other loved ones. We need to treat them the way we would want to be treated. Remember, when we're planting faithfulness, we're planting seeds. And those seeds will grow and produce an abundant harvest.

Another important aspect of faithfulness is our willingness to do the menial tasks. We should never consider ourselves too good to do anything. I truly believe that a man or woman who is not willing to clean toilets in the church restrooms or change diapers in the nursery is not prepared for a leadership role in the church.

Many years ago when my husband was an associate pastor, it was his responsibility to tar the church roof to keep it from leaking. For some reason, that roof always seemed to need repairs right in the middle of the hot, Texas summer. It wasn't much fun for Ken to be on top of the roof, pouring hot tar, with the summer sun glaring down on him. And it certainly didn't seem to be a very spiritual task. But if my husband had not been willing to tar the roof of the church, God could not have used him in the position he's in today.

You see, as soon as you begin to think, *That job is beneath my dignity,* you're already headed downhill in your spiritual growth. I still do things in the ministry today that are really someone else's responsibility. Why? Because I want to make sure I stay humble. I purposely do those things so I will keep a servant's heart.

I remember something that happened a few years ago at RHEMA Bible Church that illustrates what I'm talking about here. One Sunday morning I was serving in the nursery, and my duties included changing diapers. While I changed the diapers on those precious little ones, I prayed over them.

I noticed one of the volunteers watching me with the strangest expression on her face, so I asked her, "Is something wrong?"

"I can't believe you're the pastor's wife and you're changing diapers," she whispered incredulously.

Then she said something that really broke my heart. She said, "You would never find my pastor's wife back home changing diapers in the nursery." That is so sad! The children are the church of the future. What better place to plant good seeds than in those precious lives?

So be willing to do the menial tasks and be faithful to do them with excellence. Whatever your hand finds to do, do it with all of your might and to the best of your ability, and God will be faithful to promote you *in His season!*

Let's look for a moment at what might have happened if some of the great characters of the Bible had decided not to be faithful. For example, where would we be if Abraham had been unfaithful in his walk with the Lord? After all, he's called the father of all those who believe (Rom. 4:11), and that includes us.

What if he had said, "Oh, God, You must be joking! You aren't *really* giving me a son, are You? After all, I'm 100 years old and my wife is 90, and she's always been barren." What kind of example would he have set for us if he had done that?

Or what if Joshua had decided not to be faithful? What if he had said, "Moses is probably going to live forever. I don't need to prepare for leadership." He wouldn't have taken the proper steps to learn how to lead the people, would he? And he would never have fulfilled God's call to lead the children of Israel into the Promised Land.

And what if Joseph had not been faithful? There he sat in Pharaoh's dungeon, interpreting dreams for his fellow inmates (Genesis chapter 40). After he had interpreted the baker's and butler's dreams, the butler was released. But he promptly forgot about Joseph!

Instead of staying faithful, what if Joseph had gotten mad and decided to have a pity party? What if he had refused to interpret Pharaoh's dream? If Joseph had not been faithful, all of Egypt, as well as his entire family, might have starved to death during the famine!

There is no substitute for faithfulness. You can't borrow it from someone else. You can't inherit it. And you can't fake it. But you can practice faithfulness every day. You can develop your faithfulness—along with the other fruit of the

Spirit—as you choose to give your whole heart in serving and obeying the Lord.

Be FRUITFUL

If you stay *focused*, *fixed*, and *faithful*, then you're going to be *fruitful*. You're going to fulfill the four F's of success. You may not see the fruit immediately. But eventually, in the right season, you will produce fruit.

Psalm 1:1–3 says, "*Blessed is the man Who walks not in the counsel of the ungodly, Nor stands in the path of sinners, Nor sits in the seat of the scornful; But his delight is in the law of the Lord, And in His law he meditates day and night. He shall be like a tree Planted by the rivers of water, THAT BRINGS FORTH ITS FRUIT IN ITS SEASON, Whose leaf also shall not wither; And whatever he does shall prosper*" (NKJV).

When a tree is planted, it doesn't bear fruit immediately, does it? It takes time for the fruit to develop and grow. The fruit is produced in the proper season.

A few years ago when we were in northern California, we saw some of the biggest trees I have ever seen in my life. They were hundreds of years old and had massive trunks. When I looked at one of those gigantic trees, it was hard for me to imagine how it could have started with a little seed planted in the ground.

As the seed began to grow, it had to be watered. It needed some sunshine, and it also had to be fed or fertilized. If you plant a fruit tree, it may need to be sprayed for insects if you want to produce a healthy crop. The tree may also need to be pruned or it will get too bushy, which could hinder the production of fruit.

That's a good description of what we experience in our walk with the Lord. First, we must plant the seed of God's Word in our hearts. Then the seed must be watered as we go to church and continue to hear the Word preached. When the Word is watered, it causes our roots to grow deep, just as the tree we read about in Psalm 1.

Next, the light of the S-O-N-shine beams upon us to make us ready for a mighty harvest. Of course, our pastor may have to prune certain areas as we listen to him preach. He may even have to spray us with the Word of God to get rid of any "insects" that are trying to attach themselves to us.

I know it's not the most comfortable experience in the world to be "sprayed for insects." And it's not always easy and pleasant to be pruned. Sometimes it hurts! But that pruning and spraying will cause us to be fruitful. And oh, how wonderful it is when we reap the harvest!

When harvest time comes, we'll bear much fruit. Why? Because we've been rooted and grounded in the Word. We've been watered and fed. And we've been pruned and sprayed.

Then, if the enemy tries to throw us a curve, we'll stand strong like the tree that's planted by the rivers of water. And when the winds of life try to blow all of our fruit to the ground, we can boldly declare, "Satan, you cannot destroy my fruit! I've stayed focused. I've stayed fixed on the Lord. I've stayed faithful. And now I'm going to be fruitful. Nothing can hinder me from bearing fruit for the Lord!"

Chapter 7

WHAT ARE YOU FOCUSING ON?

Let me ask you a question today concerning your personal focus in life. If you looked at yourself honestly, would you say you were an optimist or a pessimist?

For example, when trouble strikes, do you immediately focus on the scripture that says, "All things work together for good to those who love the Lord" (Rom. 8:28)? Or do you wring your hands and cry out, "Oh dear Lord, why is this happening to me?"

Are you always focused on the difficulties that confront you or are you constantly looking for the bright side of every situation? An optimist sees the glass as half full, while a pessimist views the same glass as half empty.

My dad used to tell the story of a man who was the meanest person in town. Almost nothing good could be said about him.

Now there was another man in that town who never said a bad word about anyone. When the man who was so mean passed away, the people in the community all wondered what the man who never said anything bad about anyone would say about this man. Finally, the moment came at the funeral when he passed by the man's casket. He paused briefly, and then he exclaimed, "My, didn't he have pretty teeth!"

When we are confronted with a negative or distressing situation, we may not see many positive things to focus on. But we can always find *something* good in any situation.

I once heard another story about a little boy who was strutting across his backyard, wearing a baseball cap and carrying a bat and ball. He boldly announced, "I'm the greatest hitter in the world!" Then he tossed the ball into the air and swung at it with all of his might. But he missed. "Strike one!" he yelled out. But that didn't discourage him.

Undaunted, he picked up the ball and repeated, "I'm the greatest hitter in the world." Then he threw the ball into the air. But when he swung at it the second time, it was strike two!

That still didn't discourage the young fellow. This time, he examined the bat and ball carefully. Then he rubbed his hands together, straightened his cap, and declared once more, "I'm the greatest hitter in the world!" He tossed the ball into the air and swung at it again. But he missed the ball for the third time. Strike three!

The boy paused for a moment to ponder the situation, and then he exclaimed, "Wow! I'm the greatest pitcher in the world!"

That little boy's circumstances hadn't changed one bit. But his optimistic attitude prompted him to give a positive focus to what had happened. He was saying, "Okay, if I'm not the greatest hitter in the world, then I must be the greatest pitcher."

You see, your attitude determines how circumstances impact your life. If you try, you can always find a way to highlight the good in a bad situation. There's an old saying— "You'll find whatever you're looking for." If you're always looking for the gloomy side of life, you're going to find it.

Of course, as we process the circumstances that occur in our lives, it's easy to focus on the wrong things. I'm no different from you. I have to decide, just as you do, to take a positive approach to life.

For example, sometimes I don't want to get up in the morning. I just want to pull the covers over my head and stay in bed, because I know what I'm going to have to face that day. That's when I declare, "This is the day that the Lord has made. I will rejoice and be glad in it" (Ps. 118:24).

I declare by faith, "This is a good day because the Lord has made this day. It's going to be a day full of sunshine. It may be cloudy or rainy outside, but there's going to be sunshine in my heart!"

Really, the world has programmed us to be negative. Just look at the news reports. News is not news unless it's bad. We've been trained to focus on the dark side of every situation.

So many times as people recount an incident I hear them say, "If only this had happened. If only I could have done that." We have to stop examining the "what if's" of life and look at what can be!

Every one of us could have a pity party for the rest of our lives if we chose to. But instead we need to declare, "I am not a victim. I am a victor!" We're victorious in life because the Word says, "... *Greater is he that is in you, than he that is in the world*" (1 John 4:4).

In Philippians 4:8, the Apostle Paul described some of the specific things we should all focus on. Here is that verse from the *New Living Translation:* "... *Fix your thoughts on what is true, and honorable, and right, and pure, and lovely, and admirable. Think about things that are excellent and worthy of praise.*"

But what do we concentrate on so much of the time? We focus on the worst and not the best, don't we?

If you continually look at your spouse's negative qualities, you'll be irritated at him or her all the time. But if you start thinking about the good things your spouse does, your attitude will change completely!

So many times I hear wives complain about their husbands—"Well, my husband doesn't do this and my husband doesn't do that!"

Then I ask them, "What are some of the good things your husband does?"

After they tell me something their husbands do, you should see the looks on their faces when I tell them, "But my husband doesn't do that." Then I add, "It's OK that my husband doesn't do that, because he's not a messy person. He always hangs up his clothes. He always puts his shoes in the closet. I never have to pick up after him. That lightens my load so I have the energy to do some of the things he doesn't do."

If we focus on all the qualities we *can* appreciate in others, it will brighten our day and help us have a more positive outlook on life. Let's look for a moment at some other things we need to focus on.

Focus on the Lord, Not on the World

When I attended church services as a young person, my full concentration was on worshipping the Lord. I wanted to hear what the minister had to say, and I had an earnest desire to hear from God.

Today most of us have our cell phones with us in church. We're so accustomed to multitasking that we send text messages during praise and worship. Or we surf the Internet or write something on Facebook while we're trying to listen to the pastor preach.

Sometimes I like to imagine what God is thinking during our services today. I'm sure He gets perturbed with us at times. He probably wants to ask us, "Are you concentrating on Me, or are you concentrating on other things?"

We all want to enjoy the blessings of the Lord and receive the desires of our hearts. We claim Mark 11:23–24, and we can recite those verses by heart. But how diligently are we seeking the Kingdom of God? How often are we putting the Lord first? The verses in Mark 11:23–24 are not going to work if we spend more time focusing on our own selfish desires than on the Lord!

Another thing that can draw us away from God instead of closer to Him is the time we spend with our families. Of course, I realize that now, more than ever, we need to take special precautions to guard our families. And we certainly need to spend time with them.

But when we're with our families, sometimes we spend too much time in unnecessary places. They may not be *wrong* places or *bad* places. But our children's lives can be so filled with natural activities that the house of God is neglected.

That grieves my heart because I know how important it is for those precious little ones to have a strong foundation in the Word of God. I know how vital it is for them to know that the Bible teaches us not to forsake the assembling of ourselves together in our church services (Heb. 10:25). They need to know the importance of making their Heavenly Father the center of their lives. We must teach our young people to seek God first!

Focus on God's Ability Instead of Your Insufficiencies

In Moses, the Bible gives us a good example of someone who learned to focus on God's ability instead of his own insufficiencies. Moses had lost his temper and killed an Egyptian because the Egyptians were treating the Hebrew slaves so harshly. When Pharaoh discovered what had happened, he tried to kill Moses. But Moses fled to the land of Midian. He married a Midianite woman and began living as a shepherd.

As we pick up the story in Exodus chapter 3, Moses was minding his own business one day when all of a sudden the angel of the Lord appeared to him in a burning bush. When

Moses walked over to look at the bush, God began talking to him. He said, "I have heard the cry of My people, and I have come to deliver them." Then the Lord added, " *'I am sending you to Pharaoh to bring my people the Israelites out of Egypt'* " (v. 10 NIV).

When Moses heard those words, he began to dwell on his insufficiencies instead of on God's ability. He said, " '. . . *Who am I, that I should go to Pharaoh and bring the Israelites out of Egypt?'* " (v. 11 NIV).

Really, I believe Moses was startled by the magnitude of what God had called him to do. In Exodus chapter 4, he told the Lord, "But God, You know I'm not an eloquent speaker. I'm slow of speech" (v. 10). Then he began to argue with the Lord.

But I want you to read what God said to Moses next— " *'Now go; I will help you speak and will teach you what to say'* " (v. 12 NIV).

That still didn't satisfy Moses. In the very next verse he replied, " *'O Lord, please send someone else to do it.'* "

At that point, God became exasperated. He told Moses, "Your brother Aaron can speak eloquently. Let him be your spokesman."

So many times we ask the Lord to use us, but when He gives us an assignment, we shrink back. We tell Him, "But God, I'm not qualified for this job. Please send somebody else!" We tend to focus on our insufficiencies instead of on God's ability. But we must always remember, if God asks us to do something, He will qualify us to do it.

One time the Lord began to deal with me about speaking before a large crowd of people. At first I considered all the ramifications of it, and then I told the Lord, "Please send somebody else. You know I can't speak!"

God was pretty rough in His response. He told me, "Lynette, if I can speak through a donkey, don't you think I can speak through you?" (He was referring to the donkey who spoke to Balaam in Numbers 22:28.) Needless to say, I got the message!

What are we supposed to focus on instead of our insufficiencies? We can focus on God's ability flowing through us. We can focus on what the Bible says in Philippians 4:13—"*I can do all things through Christ* [through God's ability] *which strengtheneth me.*" Whatever God asks us to do in life, we can focus on His ability and do the task in His strength.

God may be speaking to you right now and telling you to do something that is really a stretch for you. In these last days, I believe the Lord wants to stretch all of us. And if we don't stretch, we're going to stagnate! I encourage you to let God stretch you into the arena He's calling you to and trust Him to empower you to do it.

Focus on God's Provision Instead of Your Lack

In Mark chapter 6, Jesus was teaching the multitudes, and when it was dinnertime there was no food for the people. In John's version of this story, Jesus asked Philip, "'*Where can we buy bread to feed all these people?*' " (John 6:5 NLT).

Verse 6 says that Jesus was actually testing Philip, because the Lord already knew what He was going to do.

Then Philip replied, " *'Even if we worked for months, we wouldn't have enough money to feed them!'* " (v. 7).

But Andrew, Simon Peter's brother, piped up, saying, " *'There's a young boy here with five barley loaves and two fish . . .'* " (v. 9). What a powerful declaration of his faith! But in the next instant, he blurted out his unbelief—" *'. . . But what good is that with this huge crowd?'* "

Have you ever started out making a strong declaration of your faith, but then your voice began to quiver and you slipped back over into the natural realm? Suddenly you began to speak out your fears and unbelief. I'm sure we've all been guilty of doing that at times.

The bottom line of this story is, the disciples were focusing on their lack, but Jesus was focusing on God's provision. Let me ask you today, what are you focusing on?

Jesus told the disciples to have the huge crowd of people sit down on the grassy slopes. The Bible says, " *. . . the men alone numbered about five thousand*" (v. 10). Then the Lord took the boy's loaves and fishes, blessed them, and gave thanks to God. After all the people had eaten their fill, there were twelve baskets of food left over!

When the disciples focused on their lack, the people remained hungry. But when Jesus focused on God's provision, the hungry multitude was fed!

I'm reminded of another story in Acts chapter 3, where Peter and John passed by a lame beggar at the Beautiful gate of the temple. What was the lame man focused on?—his lack of money!

But Peter and John were confident they had something that could help this man a whole lot more than money. They had the mighty Name of Jesus.

Peter said to the lame man, ". . . *Silver and gold have I none; but such as I have give I thee: In the Name of Jesus Christ of Nazareth rise up and walk*" (v. 6). And the man rose up—walking, leaping, and praising God! He received a miracle because the disciples didn't focus on their lack. They focused on God's abundant provision.

You may be focused right now on all the things you *don't* have. I urge you to focus on what you *do* have. Focus on all the blessings God has already provided for you. It will lift your spirits and help you receive the miracles you need from the Lord!

Focus on God's Delivering Power
Instead of the Circumstances

In Exodus chapter 14, we see the Israelites fleeing from the wrath of Pharaoh. Instead of focusing on God's delivering power, they were focused on the army that was trying to capture them. They were focused on the negative circumstances that were chasing them. And they began to grumble to Moses, "Have you brought us out here in the wilderness to die? Why didn't you leave us back in Egypt?"

Doesn't that sound like something we might say today? We get all hyped up in our faith when we hear someone preach a great faith message, and we immediately set out to conquer the world. Then we encounter some type of negative circumstances, and we begin to panic. We think, *Oh no! I was sure God was going to deliver us, but maybe He isn't!*

If He said He would deliver us, then He will deliver us. But sometimes our deliverance doesn't come overnight. And sometimes it requires a fight of faith.

Moses answered the people with a statement of his faith. He said, " '*Do not be afraid. Stand still, and see the salvation of the Lord. . . . For the Egyptians whom you see today, you shall see again no more forever. The Lord will fight for you, and you shall hold your peace*' " (Exod. 14:13–14 NKJV).

Moses said, "Do not be afraid." Let me tell you, the circumstances of life can scare the wits out of you. They can make you shake in your boots. But the most important thing to remember when negative circumstances arise is to *not be afraid*!

How many times in the Bible do we find the words *fear not*? God continually reminds us not to be afraid. Why? Because fear is the enemy's most effective tactic.

Do you realize what fear does to you? It grips your whole being—physically and emotionally. It paralyzes you. It can make you literally sick to your stomach. Your body begins to malfunction when you're gripped with fear.

But these verses from the Book of Exodus encourage us not to get into a state of fear. And they also give us a powerful promise from the Lord. He declared, "I will fight for you!" He was saying, "The circumstances surrounding you are nothing for Me!"

So many times we try to fight our own spiritual battles, but God is saying, "Stand still and see what I will do." God does a much better job of fighting our battles than we ever could.

What happened to Moses and the children of Israel? As soon as they began to focus on the Lord instead of their circumstances, God divided the waters of the sea and they walked across on dry land. When the Egyptians tried to follow them into that dry seabed, the waters came crashing down on them and they drowned!

Keep Your Eyes on the Rock

When I think about how important it is for us to focus on the right things, I'm reminded of a story I heard about two men who were crossing a mountain range on horseback. When they came to a large and swiftly flowing river, the older and more experienced man said to the younger one, "When we get to the deepest, swiftest part of the river, don't look down at the swirling water. If you do, it's going to make you dizzy. You're going to lose your focus."

Then the older man added, "See that big rock on the other side of the river? Keep your eyes focused on that rock. When things are swirling all around you, if you keep your eyes on the rock, you'll make it to the other side."

So they began to cross the river, but when they got out into the middle of those swift and turbulent waters, the horses began to panic. The water was spraying their faces and the current was threatening to drag them under.

All at once, the young man got nervous and began to look at the water swirling angrily around him. He lost his focus on the rock and became dizzy. He began to struggle, but the older man cried out, "Keep your eyes on the rock!"

Suddenly, the younger man came to his senses. With great effort, he focused his eyes on the rock again. When he did, he guided his horse safely to the other side of the river.

Let me give you a word of encouragement today. The circumstances of life may be making you dizzy. The problems may be swirling all around you. But if you will keep your faith focused on the Rock—the Lord Jesus Christ—it doesn't matter what kind of circumstances you're facing. God will be right there to deliver you—and not out of just one or two circumstances, but out of them *all*!

Chapter 8

NONE OF THESE THINGS MOVE ME

There's a verse in Acts chapter 20 that I encourage you to commit to memory and always endeavor to live by. Let's read the two preceding verses so you can see exactly what the Apostle Paul was experiencing when he wrote these powerful words.

ACTS 20:22–24

22 And now, behold, I go bound in the spirit unto Jerusalem, not knowing the things that shall befall me there:

23 Save that the Holy Ghost witnesseth in every city, saying that bonds and afflictions abide me.

Now here's the verse I want to highlight for you:

24 BUT NONE OF THESE THINGS MOVE ME. . . .

I pray that these words will be indelibly impressed upon your mind and heart. Why? Because so many things in this life will try to move you. The devil will use many things to try to shake you up and get you off track. You will have many opportunities in your lifetime to say, "It's just not worth it." But it's during those times that you will have to stand strong and declare by faith, "None of these things move me!"

You see, you're not always going to have someone to give you a booster shot or pat you on the back and assure you, "It's going to be all right. You can make it through this."

No, there will be times when you're out in the middle of nowhere, facing the fiery darts of the enemy, with no one but your wife or husband and your friendly dog at your side. That's when you're going to have to stir yourself up to pray. You're going to have to stir yourself up to believe God. And if you want to be successful in your Christian walk, you must not allow yourself to be moved by those things.

Paul goes on to say in verse 24, "... *neither count I my life dear unto myself, so that I might finish my course with joy....*" Notice that it's important for us not just to finish the race God has set before us, but to finish our course with joy!

Of all the people in the Bible, the Apostle Paul is the one I enjoy studying about the most. I love to read his writings because I see in him so many characteristics I admire and also things that inspire me.

Everything Paul did, he did with all of his might. He put his whole heart into whatever he was doing. And if you're going to be a success in life, it's important for you to do whatever you do with all of your might—to put your whole spirit, soul, and body into it.

When Saul of Tarsus persecuted the Christians, he did it with all of his might. And when he became Paul and joined those whom he had persecuted, he served God wholeheartedly—with all of his might! I think that's an important example for you and me to follow.

You see, our life as a Christian is a journey of faith. Faith is what the Lord requires of us. In fact, God demands that every step of the way be a step of faith.

Meanwhile, the enemy constantly tries to discourage us, just as he tried to discourage Paul. He talks to our minds, and sometimes he even plays havoc with our thoughts. He does everything in his power to try to block us from finishing the race God has set before us.

But let me tell you, when the enemy tries to bring discouragement, you must set your face like flint and determine in your heart that Satan will not succeed. He will not deter you. He will not stop you from fulfilling God's call.

How are we supposed to deal with the attacks of the devil? First Peter 5:8 says, *"Be careful—watch out for attacks from Satan, your great enemy. He prowls around like a hungry, roaring lion, looking for some victim to tear apart"* (TLB).

Satan wants to tear each and every one of us apart. He wants to tear our lives apart. He wants to tear our families, our health, and our financial situations apart. And ultimately, he's trying to tear God's Kingdom *down.* He wants to pluck everyone he can from the Kingdom of God and take them captive in his kingdom.

Sometimes the battles are fierce, and sometimes it seems as if we're dealing with a barrage of battles. But what does the Word say in First Peter 5:9? *"Stand firm when he [Satan] attacks. Trust the Lord; and remember that other Christians all around the world are going through these sufferings too"* (TLB).

What should we do when the enemy is attacking us—when he's whispering his lies in our ears? First of all, we need to speak the Word of God to Satan. When Jesus was tempted by the devil in the wilderness, what did He do? He said to Satan, "...*It is written*..." (Matt. 4:4). He answered the devil's attacks with the Word. And we must learn to combat the devil's attacks the same way Jesus did—by speaking the Word of God.

When Satan is whispering in my ears, I've discovered that it's impossible for me to listen to him if I'm quoting the Word. So when the enemy starts talking to me, I simply quote God's Word to him, just as Jesus did!

Something else I do when the devil begins to taunt me is to remind myself of my calling from the Lord. Romans 11:29 says, *"For the gifts and calling of God are without repentance."* *The Amplified Bible* puts it this way: *"For God's gifts and His call are irrevocable. [He never withdraws them when once they are given, and He does not change His mind about those to whom He gives His grace or to whom He sends His call.]"* I really like that!

That means God has not changed His mind about you. It doesn't matter what His divine call is upon your life—whether it's a call to business, to the teaching profession, or to the ministry. Don't ever underestimate His calling.

When the enemy comes in like a flood, remember God's calling. And if you don't know what God has called you to do, just remember that He has called you, first and foremost, to be His child. You're in the most important service there is—the service of the Lord Jesus Christ!

He's called you out of darkness into His marvelous light (1 Peter 2:9). He's called you into the Kingdom of His dear Son (Col. 1:13). In other words, God has called you to be a Christian, and what a great calling that is! Reminding yourself of your calling in Christ will help you say with boldness and conviction, "None of these things move me," no matter how much the enemy attacks.

No More Pity Parties

There may be times when you find yourself tempted to have a pity party. But I believe it will help you resist that temptation if you look at the circumstances that continually plagued Paul's life.

He was beaten with rods. He was run out of town. He was stoned and left for dead on the side of the road. He was thrown into prison. And what did he do? From his prison cell, he wrote, *"Rejoice in the Lord always: and again I say, Rejoice"* (Phil. 4:4).

I have visited the site in Rome where they say Paul was imprisoned. It wasn't an inspiring place to be. In fact, it was a horrible dungeon!

As I looked around in that dark, depressing dungeon, I couldn't help but think of the writings of Paul where he said, *"Rejoice in the Lord always: and again I say, Rejoice. . . . Be careful for nothing; but in every thing by prayer and supplication with thanksgiving let your requests be made known unto God. And the peace of God, which passeth all understanding, shall keep your hearts and minds through Christ Jesus"* (Phil. 4:4, 6–7).

As I stood there thinking of those verses, I wondered, *Would I have been at peace in that prison? Could I have written a letter to our RHEMA Bible Church congregation saying, "Rejoice in the Lord always: and again I say, Rejoice"?*

Could you have done those things if you had been in Paul's shoes, not knowing what the future held? Could you have rejoiced, not having any idea what was going to happen to you while you were in prison . . . or whether you were ever going to get out?

What else did Paul write from that dismal prison cell? *". . . For I have learned, in whatsoever state I am, therewith to be content"* (Phil. 4:11). And he also penned the scripture I live by every day of my life—Philippians 4:13—*"I can do all things through Christ who strengthens me"* (NKJV).

If we had penned the Book of Philippians from that jail cell, most of us would probably have written, "Grumble in the Lord always, and again I say, Grumble!" And we might have been tempted to have a pity party.

We might have cried out to the Lord, "Oh God, we've dedicated our lives to You. We've done all that You told us to do. And now look what's happened to us! Here we are in jail, and we don't really feel like rejoicing. As a matter of fact, we feel like grumbling about this whole situation. We've decided we're going to have a great, big pity party!"

Yet as Paul sat there in prison, with all the circumstances of life swirling around him, he boldly declared, *"Rejoice in the Lord always!"* He didn't say to rejoice only when everything is going right. He didn't say to rejoice when you feel you're on top of the world. He said to rejoice always, under all circumstances, no matter what!

You may feel as if you're imprisoned by your circumstances right now. But if you begin to rejoice in the Lord, those prison doors will burst wide open. Why? Because praise always reaches the very heart of God.

When your mind is giving you trouble, rejoice in the Lord. When everything around you seems to be in havoc, rejoice in the Lord. As you rejoice, God's peace will come to your mind and heart. The Holy Spirit will begin to comfort you, encourage you, and give you strength. Then you can boldly declare as the Apostle Paul declared, "None of these things move me!"

You see, that's the place where you have to be in your walk with the Lord if you want to finish your course with joy. You must proclaim to the devil and all of his henchmen, "I don't care how you endeavor to attack me. Nothing you're bringing against me will move me. I put you on notice that no matter what you do, I will rejoice!"

Full of the Word and the Spirit

How can you be so determined and dogmatic in your faith that you're not moved by the devil's attacks? It's important, first of all, for you to build yourself up in the Word. You must keep yourself full of the Word of God at all times. When that Word is hidden in your heart, it's going to come forth in the time of crisis.

Someone once said, "You can't build a foundation in the midst of a flood." That's why you need to stay tanked up on the Word of God at all times and ready for battle. You see, the enemy is sneaky. He'll wait until your tank is half full and then he'll launch his attack. But don't give him the opportunity!

It's also absolutely vital that you build yourself up by praying in the Holy Ghost (Jude 20). Perhaps you've never spoken in tongues. Maybe you've never received the baptism in the Holy Spirit. It's difficult to be victorious in this life without the power of the Holy Spirit.

Not only do you need to receive the initial infilling of the Holy Spirit and speak in tongues, but you need to keep yourself built up in the Spirit by speaking in tongues *continually*. I'll share in more detail about this subject in chapter 12.

If we want to withstand the attacks of the devil, we must be filled with the Word of God and the power of the Spirit. Psalm 118:10–14 gives us a strong word from God's Word to help us stand our ground when the enemies are roaring all around us.

PSALM 118:10–14 (TLB)

10 Though all the nations of the world attack me, I will march out behind his [God's] banner and destroy them.

11 Yes, they surround and attack me; but with his flag flying above me I will cut them off.

12 They swarm around me like bees; they blaze against me like a roaring flame. Yet beneath his flag I shall destroy them.

13 You did your best to kill me, O my enemy, but the Lord helped me.

14 He is my strength and song in the heat of battle, and now he
has given me the victory.

Let those words from the Book of Psalms ring in your
heart every time you face an attack from the enemy!

If you're filled with the Word when the devil attacks, out
of your mouth will come, "God always gives me the victory
through my Lord Jesus Christ" (1 Cor. 15:57). Out of your
mouth will come, "God always causes me to triumph in
Christ" (2 Cor. 2:14).

When you're attacked by a terminal disease and the doc-
tors have told you that you have only a short time to live, out
of your mouth will come Psalm 91:16—"God satisfies me
with long life and shows me His salvation."

When you're overwhelmed with debt and your checking
account is empty, out of your mouth will come, "But my God
shall supply all my needs, according to His riches in glory by
Christ Jesus" (Phil. 4:19). I like the way that verse reads in
The Amplified Bible: *"And my God will liberally supply (fill to
the full) your every need. . . ."* I always rejoice when I read
those words!

When your enemies are crowding around you and you're
dodging the fiery darts of the devil, out of your mouth will
come, "No weapon that's formed against me shall prosper"
(Isa. 54:17).

That's how you keep from being moved by the devastat-
ing circumstances of life. That's how you can rejoice in the
Lord always!

Adverse circumstances come to all of us. What we do with those circumstances determines the outcome of our lives. We can choose to let them move us and shake us up. Or we can refuse to allow the circumstances of life to defeat us and keep us from our destination.

It's true that we don't always understand the things that happen to us. But whatever lies before you, whatever course you may take, determine right now in your heart that you will never stray from God's path. You will not veer to the right or to the left. You will not let the enemy draw you off course. You will walk with the Lord fully, wholly, and uprightly all the days of your life.

And when Satan launches his attacks, you will stand tall and declare by faith, "None of these things move me! I've made up my mind to follow the Lord. I'm lifting my face to Heaven as I speak the Name of Jesus. I've purposed in my heart that I will finish my course with joy!"

Chapter 9

KEEP YOUR GUARD UP

In the hour in which we live, it's more important than ever for us to set a watch against the devil's plots and strategies. Never before have I seen such harassment from the enemy. If we want to accomplish what God has called us to do, we must keep our guard up against Satan at all times.

There's a dramatic story in the Book of Nehemiah that illustrates how the children of Israel set a watch against their enemies while they rebuilt the broken-down walls of Jerusalem. At the beginning of this book, Nehemiah inquired of his brother Hanani and several other men of Judah, "How are things going for the Jews in Jerusalem?"

His brother told him about the sad state of affairs in their beloved city. He said, "The walls are still torn down and the gates are burned." When Nehemiah heard that terrible report, he began to weep. Let's look at Nehemiah 1:4–6:

NEHEMIAH 1:4-6

4 And it came to pass, when I heard these words, that I sat down and wept, and mourned certain days, and fasted, and prayed before the God of heaven,

5 And said, I beseech thee, O Lord God of heaven, the great and terrible God, that keepeth covenant and mercy for them that love him and observe his commandments:

6 Let thine ear now be attentive, and thine eyes open, that thou mayest hear the prayer of thy servant. . . .

Then Nehemiah began to pray a beautiful prayer for the Jews in Jerusalem, pleading their cause before the Lord. He said, in essence, "God, I know we haven't always obeyed Your commandments, but please have mercy upon us." In verse 10 he continued, *"Now these are thy servants and thy people, whom thou hast redeemed by thy great power, and by thy strong hand."*

Nehemiah was cupbearer to the king of Persia, and the king could discern from Nehemiah's countenance that something was troubling him. He had always been smiling before, but all of a sudden, he was downcast. So the king asked him what was wrong. Nehemiah replied, "O king, it's impossible for me to be happy when my people are suffering as they are."

Then the king asked him, "What do you want to do?"

Of course, God had already been dealing with Nehemiah's heart about helping his people in Jerusalem. So he asked the king if he could go to Jerusalem and rebuild the wall. The king gave him his blessing and sent him back to Judah with a royal guard and provisions to rebuild the walls of the city.

The Attack Came Through Words

When Nehemiah returned to Jerusalem, he rallied the people to rebuild the broken-down walls. But some of their enemies heard what they were doing and became furious! They desperately tried to stop the work from going forward. Let's read the account in Nehemiah chapter 4.

NEHEMIAH 4:1-2 (NIV)

1 When Sanballat heard that we were rebuilding the wall, he became angry and was greatly incensed. He ridiculed the Jews,

2 and in the presence of his associates and the army of Samaria, he said, "What are those feeble Jews doing? Will they restore their wall? Will they offer sacrifices? Will they finish in a day? Can they bring the stones back to life from those heaps of rubble—burned as they are?"

So Nehemiah's enemies tried *through words* to destroy the work he was doing. And when you strive to accomplish what God has called you to do, you may be criticized just as Nehemiah was. You may hear someone say, "What do they think they're doing? Do they think they're somebody special?" And so many times when people criticize us, we draw back.

When Kenneth Hagin Ministries first began to proclaim the faith message, people were being set free all over the world. Our critics lashed out at us, saying we were teaching heresy. I'm sorry to say that we weren't as bold in our preaching the faith message for a season.

In some cases, we tried to answer our critics. But do you know what? We don't have to answer our critics. All we have to do is answer to the Lord. Praise God, we picked the banner of faith back up and declared boldly, "We're going to preach the truth of God's Word!"

Sanballat's words didn't stop the people in Jerusalem from rebuilding the walls of the city. When their work was half finished, their enemies became even more incensed.

They couldn't destroy the work by their words, so what did they do? Let's look at the account.

NEHEMIAH 4:7–8 (NIV)

7 But when Sanballat, Tobiah, the Arabs, the Ammonites and the men of Ashdod heard that the repairs to Jerusalem's walls had gone ahead and that the gaps were being closed, they were very angry.

8 They all plotted together to come and fight against Jerusalem and stir up trouble against it.

But Nehemiah gathered the people around him and said, *"Nevertheless we made our prayer to our God, and because of them we set a watch against them day and night"* (v. 9 NKJV). So they prayed first, and then they set a watch against their enemies day and night. Nehemiah 6:15 says they finished rebuilding the walls of Jerusalem in only 52 days!

Set a Watch

What Nehemiah experienced reminds me of what we sometimes go through in our own spiritual walk. We're trying with all of our might to build the Kingdom of the Lord Jesus Christ. But our enemies are tugging at us on every side.

The devil would like nothing better than to destroy us—to destroy leaders, churches, families, and individuals. He wants to keep each and every one of us from fulfilling the plan of God for our lives.

What must we do? First of all, we must pray. Second, we must work. And third, we must set a watch against our enemies.

This story shows us clearly that Nehemiah was a man of prayer. If we want to learn from his example, we must pray, pray, pray! And we must also let the devil know we mean business when we pray. James 5:16 says, *"The earnest (heartfelt, continued) prayer of a righteous man makes tremendous power available [dynamic in its working]"* (Amplified).

On the other hand, we don't need to pray eloquent prayers. God is not concerned about how beautiful our prayers are. All He cares about is that we pray fervently from our hearts.

Notice that Nehemiah and the Jews were praying for something specific—their protection. They knew what they wanted and they asked for it in a definite way. We need to be specific about what we ask for when we pray.

As you study this story, you'll also discover that Nehemiah's prayer was saturated with faith. Our prayers must always be saturated with faith. And prayer came before anything else for Nehemiah. Not only that, but he prayed a continued prayer. He prayed every step of the way as he worked to accomplish what God had called him to do.

But as Nehemiah and those who were helping him prayed, they carefully set a watch against their enemies. The Bible says they held their weapons in one hand while they worked with the other hand.

So many times we forget to set those watches against the enemy. We forget to keep our weapons ready. We let our guard down when we pray.

Of course, we can't just put up our fists and fight a physical battle against the devil. God has given us spiritual weapons to help us fight against the principalities and powers of darkness. (See Eph. 6:10–18.) But we need to set a watch *continually* against the forces of the enemy that would try to hinder our prayers.

For example, if we don't receive an instant answer when we pray, we must set a watch against discouragement. Instead of giving up, we need to keep on praying. We must keep on asking, seeking, and knocking, as Jesus said in Matthew 7:7 (NLT).

If you have a tendency to get your feelings hurt easily, you can set a watch against offense. You need to keep your guard up and make up your mind that you're not going to allow Satan to cause you to get your feelings hurt.

If you're prone to depression, you can set a watch against that. Don't let the enemy depress you. If you've lost a loved one or suffered any other kind of loss, set a watch against grief. Refuse to let grief overtake you.

And then there's the temptation to talk negatively about people in leadership positions in the church. Set a watch against criticism and refuse to participate in that.

It doesn't matter if someone is talking about a head usher, an associate pastor, a minister of music, a pastor's wife, or a senior pastor. We are all human and we all make mistakes. But Jesus said, *"Judge not, that you be not judged"* (Matt. 7:1 NKJV). And Psalm 105:15 tells us, *"Touch not mine anointed, and do my prophets no harm."*

Above all, we need to be sensitive to what the Spirit may be telling us, individually, to guard against. Several years ago, the heads of two major ministries in our area suffered a terrible loss when their houses burned to the ground. In one of the ministers' homes the fire was so intense that they almost didn't get all of their children out safely.

When the second fire occurred, I immediately said, "This is no coincidence. It's the work of the enemy." And my husband and I set a watch against a potential attack on our home by praying for God's protection.

Some time later we were awakened by a call from our alarm company, telling us our smoke detector was going off. We could smell smoke, and it smelled like an electrical fire. As we searched the house for the source of the smoke, it came to my remembrance how we had prayed for our home to be protected.

Finally we discovered that the fan motor in our furnace had burned out. But instead of igniting a fire, the flames had just sputtered out. I firmly believe our house was spared because we set a watch against the devil's assignment.

You might ask, "Do we need to set a watch continually?" Yes, we do! Do you think the enemy is going to tell us when he's ready to launch an attack? Absolutely not!

In fact, most of the time when the enemy comes, it's when we're having a victory party. Everything is going so well, and then—*boom*—Satan strikes out of nowhere.

We must set a watch against the enemy day and night. There is never, ever a time when we can let our guard down.

We must constantly be aware of the devil's tactics. They're usually not blatant—he can be very sly and secretive.

We must also bind together with other believers, working together for the Kingdom of God and setting a watch against Satan's onslaught. When we're united, we cannot fail!

As we set our faces like flint, we can declare, as Nehemiah did, "Our God will fight for us. Our God is going to see us through every obstacle Satan throws across our path. And as we all work together for the cause of Jesus Christ, we will scatter the forces of the devil and be a mighty force for the Kingdom of God!

Chapter 10

YOUR WORLD IS FORMED BY YOUR WORDS

Did you know that you can speak yourself into a powerful position of victory? That's because the words you speak have tremendous creative power.

Joshua 1:8 says, "*This book of the law* [God's Word] *shall not depart out of thy mouth; but thou shalt meditate therein day and night, that thou mayest observe to do according to all that is written therein: for then thou shalt make thy way prosperous and then thou shalt have good success.*"

Notice that this verse says the Word of God must not depart out of our mouths. That means we must speak the Word at all times.

Really, I don't know where I would be without the Word of God. His Word is what has kept me throughout my life. When trials come, when tests come, when tribulations come—no matter what comes—I always go to the Word of God.

Something I've observed in Christian circles today that troubles me is that many people don't seem to have a foundation of sticking with God's Word. As long as everything is going well and everyone is healthy and blessed, people are ready to serve the Lord with all of their hearts.

But when the tests and trials come, when the having-done-all–to-stand time comes, they suddenly forget about God's Word. They falter and fly away, leaving behind the only foundation that can support them through the storms of life—the Word of God.

You see, we must build a strong foundation in God's Word and stand firm on that foundation, especially when trials and troubles strike. When we hear a report that's not what we desire, we must ask ourselves, "Whose report do I believe?" Then we need to declare our faith in the report of God's Word.

Start Your Day With the Word

Before I get out of bed in the morning, I begin to make my confessions of God's Word. First I declare, "This is the day that the Lord hath made. I will rejoice and be glad in it" (Ps. 118:24). This is especially important for me because I'm not a morning person by nature, unless you're talking about 2 o'clock in the morning! I come alive around midnight, which means I'm usually wide awake when everyone else is asleep.

So it's absolutely vital for me to confess each day that "this is the day that the Lord hath made. I choose to rejoice and be glad in it." Oh yes, my body may be a little tired at times. I may not have had as much sleep as I really needed. But I speak to my body and say, "Body, you will rejoice! You will have energy. You will do what is necessary for you to do."

I refuse to allow the words "I'm so tired" to ever come out of my mouth. Why? Because I know that my world is formed by the words I speak—by my confessions. That means the more I say I'm tired, the more tired I'm going to be. And I have too much to do to be tired!

Sometimes it frustrates me when I hear people who are so much younger than I am say, "Oh, I'm so tired."

I remind them, "If you start saying you're tired now, you won't be able to get out of your chair when you're my age!"

When my energy level seems low, I choose to speak words of faith. I speak God's Word over my body. I declare, "I go in the strength of the Lord. His strength dwells in me. I'm not getting weaker. I'm getting stronger."

If I'm facing late hours or a lack of time for sleep, I confess God's Word over my sleep. I say, "Lord, I thank You that You give Your beloved sweet sleep. I thank You that You're redeeming the time that I have to sleep. I am resting in You, and I will be strengthened in You when I awake."

After I wake up, I declare, "The same Spirit that raised Christ from the dead dwells in me and quickens my mortal body" (Rom. 8:11). When I speak that verse by faith, God quickens and energizes my body, and I receive supernatural strength from the Lord!

You see, I'm using my words to create something in my life. I'm using my words to create a long, healthy life—a productive life. I'm using my words to create a life that's totally filled with strength and energy from my Heavenly Father.

Sometimes people ask me, "What kind of vitamins do you take?" I do take some vitamins, but the most important vitamins I take are my spiritual "vitamins"—praying in the Spirit, reading God's Word, attending church services, and being strengthened in the Lord. Those are the "vitamins" that will give you energy like you've never experienced before. And remember, you're giving your body a little booster shot every time you speak God's Word!

Don't Go Into Battle With Your Mouth Closed

When you're facing a spiritual battle, you should never go into that battle with your mouth closed. Your most powerful weapon against the enemy is God's Word coming out of your mouth!

In Ephesians chapter 6, the Apostle Paul described the armor God has given us to fight our spiritual battles. Verse 17 talks about our greatest offensive weapon—the sword of the Spirit—which is the Word of God. But God's Word doesn't become a sword until you speak it out of your mouth!

When you declare, "No weapon that's formed against me shall prosper" (Isa. 54:17), the Holy Spirit, the angels of God, and the Lord Jesus Christ go to work on your behalf. Jeremiah 1:12 (Amplified) tells us that God watches over His Word to perform it. As you speak God's Word by faith, your words become the sword of the Spirit, and your sword will destroy all the attacks of the devil.

Of course, you may have to declare the Word more than once before your confessions become a reality. But if you want to win the good fight of faith, you cannot give up.

It takes toughness. It takes tenacity. In the midst of whatever you may be going through, it takes boldness to keep speaking the Word and saying, "I'm going *through!*"

I don't know about you, but I've decided to go *through* the trials and troubles of life. I've decided I'm going to receive all God has intended for me. Many times we fall short of the blessings of the Lord because we don't press in and by faith take hold of what He has promised us. When it looks as if God's Word is not working, we stop confessing it.

What would have happened to the woman with the issue of blood if she hadn't pressed in to receive her miracle (Mark chapter 5)? What if she had stopped confessing her faith when she saw the huge crowd surrounding Jesus?

I'm sure she must have been gripped with fear when she reached out to touch the hem of Jesus' garment. After all, she wasn't supposed to be out in public. She was considered unclean because of the blood condition that plagued her body. And she was also weak physically. She had suffered from that issue of blood for 12 years!

What if she had said, "I'm just too weak. This is too hard. I'll never make it"? What if she had turned back? She would never have received her healing.

But what did she do? She kept on pressing through the crowd. And she kept on speaking out her faith. Mark 5:28 says, "*SHE KEPT SAYING, If I only touch His garments, I shall be restored to health*" (Amplified).

It's so important for us to *keep saying* what God's Word says about the problems we face. Why? Because our world is being formed by our words. If we speak words of doubt, fear, and unbelief, that's exactly what we're going to have. But if we speak God's Word and continue to speak it, we're going to have what His Word promises us!

The woman in Mark chapter 5 kept saying, "If I can only touch His garments, I will be restored to health." She was forming her world by her words. Then she began to do something—she began to act on her faith. She pressed through the large crowd that was thronging the Lord. Next she reached out and grabbed the hem of Jesus' garment, just as she had said in faith over and over again. And she was healed! Her world was transformed by her words.

Can you see from this woman's story why it's so important for you to speak God's Word continually? Can you see how her bold confession of faith dramatically changed her life?

I admonish you today—when you're discouraged, speak the Word of God. When you need finances, speak the Word of God. When you experience family problems, speak the Word of God. When you're struck with symptoms in your body, speak the Word of God.

As you continue to speak the Word and obey the commandments of the Lord, you'll create a different kind of world, a different kind of future. It will be an exciting and adventurous world—a world where your confessions of faith will become a reality!

PART III

---❧---

RELATIONSHIP

Your Connection With God and Man

Chapter 11

---∽∾---

DO YOU KNOW HIM?

The number one desire—*the greatest desire*—of our Heavenly Father is that we *know* Him. Many of us know Him as Savior, but God doesn't want our relationship to end there. He desires to communicate with us on so many levels—to guide us and give us wisdom no matter what we're going through in life. Whatever we need, God wants to be there for us—as our Healer, Provider, Counselor, and best Friend.

In the natural, there are different degrees of knowing people. I could say that I know my local congressman, but I don't actually know him very well. On the other hand, after more than 40 years of marriage and daily communication with my husband, I can truly say that I *know* my husband. We know each other so well that much of the time we don't have to exchange words to communicate. We already know what the other person is thinking. Why? Because we have spent so much time together!

That's how we need to be with our Father God. The more time we spend in His presence, communicating with Him, the more our thoughts and ways will line up with His thoughts and ways. His desires will become our desires.

Why must we know Him? Daniel 11:32 says, ". . . *the people that do know their God shall be strong, and do exploits.*"

The Amplified Bible says that the people who know their God *". . . shall prove themselves strong and shall stand firm and do exploits [for God]."* To be strong, to be able to stand firm—especially in these last days—we must know our God.

Daniel—A Man Who Knew His God

Daniel was a man who knew His God. He was a mighty man of prayer and also a man of excellence (Dan. 6:3). Even though Daniel was a captive in the land of Babylon, he had great favor with King Darius—so much so that *". . . the king thought to set him over the whole realm"* (Dan. 6:3). Daniel's favor with the king did not go unnoticed by the other rulers. They were jealous of him and consulted together to establish a royal statute against him.

DANIEL 6:7-9 (NKJV)

7 All the governors of the kingdom, the administrators and satraps, the counselors and advisors, have consulted together to establish a royal statute and to make a firm decree, that whoever petitions any god or man for thirty days, except you, O king, shall be cast into the den of lions.

8 Now, O king, establish the decree and sign the writing, so that it cannot be changed, according to the law of the Medes and Persians, which does not alter."

9 Therefore King Darius signed the written decree.

These men knew it was Daniel's custom to pray three times a day to his God (Dan. 6:10). When they could find no fault with him, they purposed in their hearts to trap him through his prayer life. The king decreed that no one could pray to anyone but the king for the next 30 days or that person would be thrown into the lions' den.

What did Daniel do? He continued to do just as he had always done—he prayed to his God.

DANIEL 6:10 (NKJV)

10 Now when Daniel knew that the writing was signed, he went home. And in his upper room, with his windows open toward Jerusalem, he knelt down on his knees three times that day, and prayed and gave thanks before his God, as was his custom since early days.

As far as Daniel was concerned, it was business as usual. Some of us would have thought, *I'm going to pray to God just as I always have, but I'm going to keep my windows closed and pray quietly.* Not Daniel! He opened his windows and prayed fervently. He believed that regardless of what happened, the God he knew would take care of him.

As he prayed, the rulers who were out to get him—those tattletales—reported him to King Darius. Though the king was upset because he loved Daniel dearly, he could not reverse his decree (Dan. 6:14–15). So he ordered that Daniel be thrown into the lions' den. But he said to Daniel, "'. . . *Your God, whom you serve continually, He will deliver you*'" (Dan. 6:16 NKJV). And God did deliver Daniel!

After spending the night with the lions, Daniel told the anxious king not to worry. "'*My God sent His angel and shut the lions' mouths, so that they have not hurt me.*'" Then he added, "'. . . *because I was found innocent before Him; and also, O king, I have done no wrong before you*'" (Dan. 6:22 NKJV).

In the middle of a den of hungry lions, Daniel could be at peace—he could rest confidently—knowing that his God would deliver him. Why could he rest and be at peace? Because he *knew* his God. He continually served him in both good times and bad—and God kept him from all harm.

Do you know your God as Daniel did? Can it be said of you that you serve your God continually? These are powerful questions, but it's time for us to know our God. It's time for us to be strong and do mighty exploits for Him!

Know the Father Through His Word

How do we know our God? First of all, we know Him through His Word. We must spend time meditating in the Word because the Word reveals the character of God.

You see, the Bible is our instruction book. We learn from God's Word what our rights are, what our authority is, how to live uprightly, and how to resist the devil. We also learn what God desires for our lives.

It's so important for us to set aside time every day to study the Word of God. So many times, the Lord will speak to us through His written Word. He'll give us instructions, comfort, and wisdom.

In my own life, there have been times when I desperately needed to hear from God, and He spoke to me clearly through His Word. When we were facing the decision to go to work for Kenneth Hagin Ministries, I struggled with making that move. In the natural, it seemed to be the wrong thing for us to do.

My husband had been in full-time pulpit ministry—preaching every week. The job his dad offered him was the position of crusade director. He would no longer be preaching. Instead, he would be taking care of the business side of the ministry. If that wasn't enough to think about, our salary was going to be cut in half. So in the natural, this move seemed to be a demotion. Yet the Lord had dealt very strongly with my husband that this was the next step we should take.

For my part, I was happy where we were. I didn't want to move! So I cried out to God, "Please show me Your plan. I have to hear from You."

I knew how important it was for me to support my husband. But I also knew that I could only be a support if I was confident in what we were doing. So I began to pray as I'd always done—but it was the driest prayer I'd ever prayed in my life. It was as if my prayers were not reaching any farther than the eight-foot ceiling in the room where I was praying! I thought, *God, this is the way You've always spoken to me before, but it doesn't seem to be working now. I'm not getting an answer.*

Then the Lord began leading me to spend extra time reading my Bible. So I started reading the Word out loud every night, and I did this for two weeks. All of a sudden a light bulb turned on in me. I realized that everything I had been reading was *by faith, by faith, by faith*. And I knew right then that my husband was right about the way we were to go. I *knew* that I *knew* that I *knew* that this was God's plan for our lives.

How vital it is that we take time to get acquainted with the Father by reading His Word. As we read the Bible, we need to ask the Lord to enlighten the eyes of our understanding (Eph. 1:18). In my own experience, when I have prayed, "Father, enlighten the Word to me," He's shown me things that I've never seen before. I've been able to walk in the truth of what He was saying to me and at the same time get to know my Heavenly Father through His Word.

Prayer: A Wireless Connection

The second way we come to know the Father is through prayer. Prayer is how we *fellowship* with Him. It's the way we talk to Him and hear His instructions for us.

In the natural, if we want to talk to someone, we call that person on the telephone. Today, most of us have cell phones, and my, how we depend on them! They allow us to communicate with almost anyone in the world at any time. However, do you realize that for thousands of years we have had a wireless connection with the most important being ever known—the King of Kings and Lord of Lords? How have we had this connection? Through prayer!

All too often, we haven't taken full advantage of our prayer connection with the Father. It's the same way with our cell phones. We can do many things on our cell phones, but we may not be using them to their fullest capacity. For example, we may struggle for 10 minutes trying to send a text message. But someone else may be able to send the same message in 30 seconds. Why? Because they have practiced sending text messages.

We wonder why some people get their prayers answered faster than others. It's because they've practiced. They're in direct communication with their Heavenly Father at all times. So many of us are living defeated lives because we have not understood how important our connection with the Heavenly Father is. He's right there to lead us, guide us, and direct us—but we have to stay connected!

Prayer Principles

James 5:16 in *The Amplified Bible* tells us, "*The earnest (heartfelt, continued) prayer of a righteous man makes tremendous power available [dynamic in its working].*" In other words, tremendous power is available to every believer! But this verse says that the power only comes through prayer, which means it takes an effort on our part.

Thankfully, there are several principles we can follow to help us commune with our Father. Number one, we must *be disciplined*. First Peter 4:7 says, "*. . . be earnest and disciplined in your prayers*" (NLT). There are only 24 hours in each day, and we must decide that prayer is a priority for us.

When it comes to praying, our intentions are usually good. We start out praying consistently, but then something interrupts our routine. Once that happens, we may find it difficult to get back into that routine.

Or maybe we've dedicated ourselves to spending a certain amount of time in prayer every day. We start out fervently, and we're so excited to pray. Then we think, *Oh, I must have prayed for at least an hour already!* But when we check the clock, it's only been ten minutes. From that point on, we're struggling.

We've all been there! I know there have been times when I've prayed and it has been dry. Thank goodness we don't go by our feelings. But I do love it when I'm inspired to pray! I love to feel close to the Lord and talk to Him just as I would a friend or someone else dear to me. That's why it's important for us to create an atmosphere in which God can speak to us—any time.

Secondly, we must *stay in God's presence on purpose.* In my own life, I want to be in direct connection with my Heavenly Father any time I need Him. Sometimes I don't have time to pray 30 minutes before I handle a situation. I need His presence with me—His wisdom—right at that moment!

As I mentioned in chapter 1, I keep myself surrounded with worship music 24 hours a day—music that opens up my heart to God and sets the atmosphere for me to pray. I play that music at night when I'm sleeping. I play it in the morning when I'm getting ready. I play it in my car when I'm driving. And when we're traveling, I even play it in the hotel room where we stay.

Wherever I am, I want to be totally saturated with the Spirit of God. I want my heart to be open to hear from the Lord any time He wants to speak to me. I'll tell you, as you open up your heart to Him, it becomes amazingly easy to pray. You'll find that you have wonderful times of prayer with your Heavenly Father!

It's so easy to pray when you're in the presence of God. And music is a powerful way to take you into His presence. I encourage you to find some music that opens up your heart and play it as much as you can. It will help you stay connected with the Lord at all times and keep you in an atmosphere to pray.

The third principle that can help us in our praying is that we must *open our mouths and talk to the Father.* This sounds so simple, but you can't develop a relationship with someone if you don't talk to them.

What would happen if you didn't say a single word to your spouse or loved one for seven days? I know what would happen in my marriage. The first day, my husband would think, *She's really tired. I'll just leave her alone.* If I woke up the second day and didn't talk to him, his next thought would be, *What have I done? How come she's not talking to me?*

By the third day, he would start taking offense. He might have tried to talk to me on the first and second days, but by day three he would stop talking. And by the seventh day, instead of growing closer in our relationship, we'd be further away from one another.

The same thing is true in our relationship with our Heavenly Father. We can't develop a strong relationship with Him unless we open our mouths and talk to Him. We don't have to use fancy words. We can just go to Him and say, "Father, this is how I feel." No matter where we are, no matter what time it is, we can talk to our Heavenly Father!

The fourth thing we can do to help us pray is *follow the leading of the Holy Spirit.* So many people get caught up in praying one particular kind of prayer, but we need to allow the Holy Spirit to lead us in praying whatever kind of prayer He wants us to pray.

There have been times when I've knelt down to pray for something very specific, but as I prayed, God led me to pray in a different area—for something I hadn't even thought about. But the Holy Spirit knows what prayer needs to be prayed.

We should learn to pray by the promptings of the Holy Ghost. We should pray because the Holy Spirit is triggering us on the inside to pray. The Holy Spirit will give us prayer impulses straight from Heaven if we're sensitive to our spirits.

Finally, we must *know the power of prayer*. Jesus did. When He was here on the earth, He did not teach His disciples how to preach. He taught them how to pray. (See Matt. 6:7–13.) Jesus knew that as the disciples communed with the Father, the Holy Spirit would teach them what they needed to know. He knew that this was the key to their success in life and ministry.

In His own life, Jesus constantly prayed to the Father. Even before He was to be crucified, Jesus prayed in the Garden of Gethsemane. Though He knew the Father well, He always took time to commune with Him. He always took time to connect with the will of the Father. As a result, He was able to accomplish the Father's will in His life.

If we ever get the revelation of how powerful our prayers are, it will be so easy to pray. Through prayer, we can enter the Throne Room of God, and it's there—in His presence—where we draw our strength. Prayer *is* the most powerful instrument we have as believers. And it's the key that unlocks the vast treasures of Heaven's power!

Your Determined Purpose

The Apostle Paul is a perfect example of someone who knew the power of prayer—someone who really knew the Lord and continually sought to know Him more. In Philippians 3:8 Paul noted, ". . . *I consider everything a loss compared to the surpassing greatness of knowing Christ Jesus my Lord, for whose sake I have lost all things. I consider them rubbish, that I may gain Christ*" (NIV). I like the way *The Amplified Bible* translates this verse.

PHILIPPIANS 3:8 (Amplified)

8 Yes, furthermore, I count everything as loss compared to the possession of the priceless privilege (the overwhelming preciousness, the surpassing worth, and supreme advantage) of knowing Christ Jesus my Lord and of progressively becoming more deeply and intimately acquainted with Him [of perceiving and recognizing and understanding Him more fully and clearly]. For His sake I have lost everything and consider it all to be mere rubbish (refuse, dregs), in order that I may win (gain) Christ (the Anointed One).

Paul *knew* his Lord, and he counted everything else as loss compared to this "priceless privilege." We see his passion again in verse 10.

PHILIPPIANS 3:10 (Amplified)

10 [For my determined purpose is] that I may know Him [that
I may progressively become more deeply and intimately
acquainted with Him, perceiving and recognizing and
understanding the wonders of His Person more strongly
and more clearly], and that I may in that same way come to
know the power outflowing from His resurrection. . . .

"For my determined purpose is that I may know Him."
Paul's determined purpose in life was to know the Lord. He
did not ask for a blessing or anything for himself. In fact,
throughout Paul's writings, he never asked for things for
himself. Instead, he boldly sought to know His Lord. He
boldly praised God and declared what He had in Christ.
*"Praise be to the God and Father of our Lord Jesus Christ, who
has blessed us in the heavenly realms with every spiritual
blessing in Christ"* (Eph. 1:3 NIV).

Again in Second Corinthians 4:1, Paul said, *"Since God
has so generously let us in on what he is doing, we're not about
to throw up our hands and walk off the job just because we
run into occasional hard times . . ."* (Message). He continued
sharing his heart later in that chapter.

2 CORINTHIANS 4:16–18 (Message)

So we're not giving up. How could we! Even though on the
outside it often looks like things are falling apart on us, on
the inside, where God is making new life, not a day goes
by without his unfolding grace. These hard times are small
potatoes compared to the coming good times, the lavish
celebration prepared for us. There's far more here than
meets the eye. The things we see now are here today, gone
tomorrow. But the things we can't see now will last forever.

Because Paul purposed to know God, he could rejoice when troubles and trials came his way. He could declare in the face of adversity, "I always triumph in Christ Jesus" (2 Cor. 2:14). Paul could be confident in every situation, knowing that *his* God—the God he had a relationship with— would always deliver him.

Until we know God as Paul did, as Daniel did, and as Jesus did, we will not be able to boldly declare, "These hard times aren't anything at all compared to what God has planned for us!" Our passion—our greatest desire—must be to know our Father.

We must diligently seek Him through the Word and fellowship with Him in prayer. We must come to know Him better than anything or anyone in this life, because when we know the Father, we know the end result. We always triumph. No matter what path our life takes, the God we know—our Heavenly Father—will get us to our destination in victory!

Chapter 12

―― ❧ ――

HEARING THE VOICE
OF THE LORD

In these last days, it's more important than ever for us to fine-tune our spiritual ears to hear the Lord's voice. God is constantly trying to speak to us. He's trying to warn us of things to come. But so many times we simply shrug it off. We think, *Oh well, that's just me.* But it's not! It's the Holy Spirit's voice!

How Do We Know When God Is Speaking to Us?

One of the difficulties I have seen in the Body of Christ today is an inability to recognize the voice of the Lord. It's extremely difficult to follow God's instructions if you don't know when He's speaking to you. Many think they are hearing God's voice when they are actually listening to the voices of others or even to the voice of their own desires.

It's so important for all of us to learn to recognize the voice of God. Remember when the Lord spoke to the boy Samuel and he did not recognize His voice? (See 1 Sam. 3:1–10.) Samuel thought the prophet Eli was calling him.

Finally Eli said to the young boy, *"Go, lie down: and it shall be, if he call thee, that thou shalt say, Speak, Lord; for thy servant heareth. So Samuel went and lay down in his place. And the Lord came, and stood, and called as at other times, Samuel, Samuel. Then Samuel answered, Speak; for thy servant heareth"* (vv. 9–10).

How do we know when God is speaking to us? Each of us has to fine-tune our spirit to hear the Holy Spirit's voice. Romans 8:14 says, *"For as many as are led by the Spirit of God, they are the sons of God."* And in Proverbs 20:27 we read, *"The spirit of man is the candle of the Lord, searching all the inward parts of the belly."* When explaining this scripture, my father-in-law would say, "The spirit of man is the light bulb of the Lord. God will enlighten us—He will guide us—through our spirits."

To be able to hear God's voice, we must set aside time to wait in His presence and allow Him to talk to us. You see, it's when we are still—when we don't have any other agenda besides worshipping and communing with the Lord—that we can hear from Him most clearly.

I remember how the prophet Elijah learned to hear the voice of the Lord. (See 1 Kings 19:11–13.) God told him to stand before Him on the mountain, and a great wind began to blow. But the Lord's voice was not in the wind. Then an earthquake shook the mountain, but the Lord was not speaking through the earthquake. Next a fire began to blaze and roar, but God's voice was not in the fire. At last, Elijah heard a still, small voice—the voice of the Lord speaking to him.

So many times in our fast-paced world, we don't get quiet enough to hear the still, small voice of God. Or we don't spend enough time communing with the Lord to be able to hear Him speak to us.

Communing with the Lord does not mean that we kneel down, pray, and say, "Okay, God, I need an answer about this situation," and then expect Him to answer us immediately. Often we get impatient in our prayer times and make up an answer ourselves and decide that it's God's answer. We head in a certain direction or make a decision and then wonder why things don't go well.

Let me ask you a question: how much time have you spent waiting on the Lord? David mastered the art of waiting on the Lord. He referred to it numerous times in his writings. Here are two examples: *"Wait on the Lord: be of good courage, and he shall strengthen thine heart: wait, I say, on the Lord"* (Ps. 27:14); and *"Wait on the Lord, and keep his way, and he shall exalt thee to inherit the land . . ."* (Ps. 37:34).

In hearing the voice of God or being led by His Spirit, I have found that God speaks to me after I have spent considerable time meditating on the matter. To put it simply, I make my request known unto God first, as the Bible says in Philippians 4:6—*"Be careful for nothing; but in every thing by prayer and supplication with thanksgiving let your requests be made known unto God."*

I state my situation in simple language, just as I would when asking someone for advice in the natural. Then I begin to thank the Lord for the answer. And I add, "Lord, help me be sensitive to Your voice when You speak."

In my prayer times after that, I briefly remind the Lord that I need an answer to my request. Often when I'm getting ready in the morning or driving in the car, I will say—sometimes out loud and sometimes in my thoughts—"Lord, You know I need to know what to do. Thank You for the answer and the solution to this problem."

Then I rest in peace. I may not have direction at the moment, but I am confident that the answer will come. I do not worry or fret about it. When I am tempted to be anxious or concerned, I simply remind the Lord that I need an answer.

That answer may come days, weeks, or even months later. I may be worshipping and praising the Lord when suddenly, out of my spirit will come thoughts that are the answer to what I have asked Him. At that moment I may not even be thinking about the request. Therefore, I know that these are not my thoughts but the thoughts of the Lord. He is enlightening my spirit and giving me the wisdom I asked Him for.

I trust this simple personal illustration will help you hear the voice of the Lord and recognize His leadings. As you learn to train your spirit to be sensitive to His voice, you will find that you will experience peace, knowing that you are walking in His divine will.

He Warns Us of Things to Come

One reason it's so important for us to be sensitive to the Spirit is that hearing from the Lord could save our lives or the lives of others. When we fine-tune our ears to hear His voice, He can warn us of things to come. John 16:13 tells us,

"Howbeit when he, the Spirit of truth, is come, he will guide you into all truth . . . and he will shew you things to come."

One day when I was driving home from work, the traffic light ahead of me had just turned green. I was in a hurry, but something on the inside of me prompted me to slow down. At first I didn't want to, because I was afraid I would miss the light. But I've learned through the years that I'd better listen to the Holy Spirit, so I began to slow down.

All of a sudden, a car barreled through the intersection right in front of me, running the red light. If I had continued going at the same speed, that car would have struck me full force. Thank God the Holy Spirit warns us of things to come!

How many times have you heard people say, "Something was telling me not to do that, but I thought it was just me"? Don't override those feelings. If you train yourself to be more sensitive to God's voice, it will keep you out of much danger and heartache.

Praying in the Spirit

Did you know that God has given us a way to pray when we don't know how to pray about a situation? Romans 8:26 says, *"Likewise the Spirit also helpeth our infirmities: for we know not what we should pray for as we ought: but the Spirit itself* [Himself] *maketh intercession for us with groanings which cannot be uttered."* That verse is talking about praying in the Spirit or praying in tongues. It's so important for us to be filled with the Spirit and practice praying in the Spirit.

If we don't pray in the Spirit, we may quickly run out of words to express our prayers to the Lord. But if we pray in the language of the Holy Spirit, we will never run out of the right words to pray.

Contrary to what you may have been told, you don't have to "tarry" to receive the Holy Spirit. When I was a girl, we tarried until we got so tired that we almost passed out before we finally received the Holy Ghost. I said "Hallelujah" and "Praise the Lord" so many times when I was trying to receive the Holy Spirit that I finally *did* pass out! Thank God, when I came to, I was speaking in tongues! Why was this experience so hard for me? Because I had no idea how to yield to the Spirit.

I remember when I first came into the Charismatic movement, I found out that you don't have to tarry to receive the Holy Ghost. All you have to do is ask the Lord and then yield to Him, and you will receive what you've asked for. It's not hard to receive the Holy Spirit!

Divine Interruptions

When we're sensitive to the Spirit, we become more aware when He's trying to interrupt us with a mission from the Lord. I remember a day when God spoke to me very bluntly about being so focused on my own to-do list.

He said, "Lynette, you're so focused on your agenda that you get irritated by the interruptions in your life. You refuse to listen to My interruptions, even though I'm endeavoring to use you through those interruptions. Interruptions are actually a more important part of your work than your to-do list is."

When He said that, I immediately had to repent. I told the Lord, "I'll do whatever You have for me to do today, and I won't complain about not being able to check the items off my to-do list. If I don't get any of my to-do list done, it will be OK as long as I've done *Your* to-do list."

I'm sure if the efficiency experts had examined Jesus' schedule, they would have said that His average day looked like a hodgepodge of unplanned activities. They would probably have told Him, "Jesus, You need to go to a time-management seminar to help You do a better job of planning Your schedule."

But what did Jesus say? "I have come to this earth to do the will of My Father" (John 6:38). Jesus' own agenda didn't matter to Him. The most important thing to Him was finding out what the *Father's* agenda was and doing it. And that should be the most important thing for us too! We should never be too busy for an assignment from God.

I remember something that happened to me at *Campmeeting* several years ago. A man we knew who had grown up in the ministry was attending *Campmeeting* that year. Little did I know the hurt inside him. He felt he would never be able to fulfill the calling God had on his life because of some mistakes he had made. And it was eating him up!

Many times when people are hurting desperately, they don't share it with anyone. So it's extremely important for us to be sensitive to the Holy Ghost so we can reach out to those people with the compassion of the Lord.

When I talked to this man, he was smiling on the outside and he said all the right things. But he was really at the point of giving up. The enemy had been telling him, "Your life is over. You might as well take your own life." And for a moment, he listened to the devil's lies.

He had told the Lord, "If You don't minister to me in this *Campmeeting,* I'm going to kill myself." He had even instructed his family concerning who he wanted to have his most treasured possessions!

When it was time for this man and his sister to leave *Campmeeting,* we said our good-byes and they went to the airport. But all of a sudden, the Spirit of God got hold of him. He told his sister, "We can't leave yet. I haven't received what I needed from the Lord."

I was so shocked when I spotted those two people coming toward me in the convention center exhibit hall. "Guys!" I exclaimed. "I thought you were already gone."

"We were," they replied. Then he added, without even a hint of urgency, "But I felt I needed to come back because the Lord wasn't through speaking to me."

Now remember, this was in the middle of *Campmeeting,* one of the busiest weeks in my life. Hundreds of people were crowding around us in the exhibit hall. But when that man said, "I felt like I needed to come back," all of a sudden— *bam*—on the inside of me I knew this was my opportunity, my time to minister. It was a divine interruption from the Lord.

Ken and I had already made plans to go to lunch with some other people. We had even made reservations. But on the inside I was listening to the Holy Ghost, and He was telling me to invite these people to go to lunch with us. So I did.

It didn't matter if we had enough reservations or not, it was going to happen!

When we arrived at the restaurant, I asked the two of them to sit right next to me. I'm not a bold person, especially to tell a man what to do. But the Spirit of God came upon me, and I told this man, "Your life is not over! There's a calling on your life, and you've got to come to RHEMA Bible Training Center."

As I talked to him, the tears began to stream down his face. I didn't even realize what I was saying because he hadn't told me that he was contemplating taking his life. But, thank God, we don't have to know the whole story to minister to someone. All we have to know is what the Holy Ghost is saying inside us.

As I talked to this man about attending RHEMA, even though he was saying yes to me, I knew he had to make some kind of commitment or he would never come. And I also knew by the Spirit that if he did not come to RHEMA, his life was over.

So I told him, "You and your sister are going with me right now, and we're going to find you an apartment." I knew if he put a deposit on an apartment and signed a lease, he would commit to coming to RHEMA.

It was raining cats and dogs that day, and I hate rain. Not only that, but I was also wearing a new pair of shoes, and I didn't want them to get ruined. But I went traipsing through the pouring rain in my brand-new shoes to help this man look at apartments. Of course, my shoes were ruined, but I didn't care because I was on a rescue mission from God!

We found that man an apartment, and he signed for it on the dotted line. He came to RHEMA that year, and it turned out that we needed his help as much as he needed ours.

You see, my husband and I started RHEMA Bible Church that fall, and we needed a good worship leader. This man had traveled all over the world with his sisters, singing in the ministry. He's an awesome musician. He has perfect pitch and a wonderful gift to lead others in worshipping the Lord. So he became our first worship leader and music minister at RHEMA Bible Church.

God restored him. He later became a pastor. And I thank God that I had even a small part in encouraging him to get back into the perfect will of God. But it never would have happened if I hadn't been sensitive to the voice of the Spirit.

I'll never forget what he said to me at *Campmeeting* a few years later. He said, "Thank you and Pastor Ken for being in the 'salvage' business and helping me at the most desperate point in my life. Everybody whose life I touch, you have a part in it!"

Did you know that God wants to send all of us on His rescue missions? And yet we're passing by some of the most amazing opportunities because we're not sensitive to what the Holy Spirit is saying to us. I encourage you to make a commitment to the Lord right now to let the Holy Ghost interrupt you any time He wants to. And you will be amazed and rejoice at the powerful way God will use you!

Who's Doing the Talking?

One of the most important things to remember if we want to hear God's voice is that He can't speak to us when we're doing the talking. He said in Psalm 46:10, *"Be still, and know that I am God...."* When we commune with our Heavenly Father, we can tell Him our thoughts, desires, needs, and wants. But then it's important for us to be quiet and let Him speak. If we're having trouble hearing God's voice, the problem may be that we're doing all the talking!

I remember one time when my father-in-law came into my office and sat down, but he didn't say anything to me. Now I tend to feel uncomfortable when it's too quiet, so I tried to strike up a conversation with him.

First, I said, "Hi, how are you?" but he didn't respond. Then I started rambling. After a few minutes, he just got up and left!

I was puzzled because Brother Hagin did not go to someone's office unless he was on a mission. So I thought, *Well, he didn't talk this time. Maybe he'll talk to me next time.*

Several weeks later, he came to my office again. I said, "Hello, how are you?" but once again he didn't respond. Being uncomfortable with the silence, I started talking again. Right in the middle of my "conversation," he abruptly got up and left my office.

This was disturbing to me because I knew he had something on his mind. At this point, I was really wondering what it was. I thought, *OK, I've failed two times, and with him, it's three strikes and you're out.* So I decided I wasn't going to fail the next time!

I immediately began to devise my plan. I decided that when he came to my office again, it didn't matter if we sat there for 30 minutes or an hour in silence, I wasn't going to say anything. I wanted to find out why he was coming to see me!

A week or two later, Brother Hagin walked into my office again, and I thought, *OK, Dad, I'm ready for you this time!* So I said, "Hello, how are you?" as I was taught in school. But that's all I said. Then I just sat back in my chair and didn't say another word!

That was probably the most uncomfortable experience I've ever had in my whole life. It seemed as if we sat there in silence for at least 30 minutes. (In reality, it was probably only five minutes.)

Then he grinned and started talking to me, and I thought he would never stop! He just kept on talking and talking. From that moment on he would always come into my office and talk freely with me. *But I had to stop talking first!*

That may be the way it is when you pray to the Father. The problem may be that you're doing all the talking and you haven't stopped long enough to hear what the Lord wants to say to you. I encourage you to practice being quiet and waiting on the Lord. You'll be amazed at how much He has to say to you!

The Crossroads

Each day of our lives we are confronted with a crossroads. It's absolutely vital for us to listen to God's voice and allow Him to direct our steps. We need to keep our ears open continually to hear from the heart of God.

We must learn to walk when He says walk and stop when He says stop. We must learn to take His path for us.

Whether you're contemplating major adjustments or minor changes, listen closely to the voice of the Lord. Open your heart to Him, and He will direct your steps.

As you wait in His presence, He will lead you and guide you. He will show you the right way to go.

The more you commune with the Lord and worship Him, the clearer His voice will be and the more specific His directions will become. He will fill your life with new purpose and give you fresh passion. He will renew your vision and give you a newness and freshness in your heart—a freshness that can only come when you hear the voice of God!

Chapter 13

---∾---

GOD EXPECTS OUR TREASURES

Do you believe you're giving God your very best gifts? That's a sobering question, isn't it? But it's one that each of us must answer if we truly want the Lord to have first place in our lives. We must give Him first place with our money—our treasures.

Let's look at the Book of Malachi, chapter 3, and I encourage you to underline these verses in your Bible.

MALACHI 3:10-12

10 Bring ye all the tithes into the storehouse, that there may be meat in mine house, and prove me now herewith, saith the Lord of hosts, if I will not open you the windows of heaven, and pour you out a blessing, that there shall not be room enough to receive it.

11 And I will rebuke the devourer for your sakes, and he shall not destroy the fruits of your ground; neither shall your vine cast her fruit before the time in the field, saith the Lord of hosts.

12 And all nations shall call you blessed: for ye shall be a delightsome land, saith the Lord of hosts.

The Word of God says, "*Bring ye all the tithes into the storehouse . . . and prove me now herewith.*" God is saying,

"Bring your tithes into My storehouse, and I will show you how abundantly I will pour out My blessings on you."

Some people would say that tithing was instituted under the law. But Abraham paid tithes before the law was ever given. (See Gen. 14:18–20.) So tithing was established before the law.

What is the tithe? The tithe is 10 percent of your income. Do all Christians obey this command to tithe? Much to my sorrow, they do not. And then they wonder why they're not blessed.

The research that's been done in this area indicates that a large number of Christians give *something* to their church. But only a small percentage actually tithe.

I saw a cartoon not long ago that illustrates the attitude many Christians have toward giving their money to the Lord. In the first frame, a man was looking at a car he was interested in buying. He asked the salesman, "What are the terms?"

The salesman replied, "Ten percent down, and low payments for 48 months."

Immediately the man replied, "Where do I sign?"

In the second frame, the same man was looking at a refrigerator on display in an appliance center. When he asked the salesman about the terms, the man told him, "Nothing down, and no interest for 12 months."

Once again the man said without hesitation, "Where do I sign?"

In the third frame, the same man was looking for a house to buy. The realtor told him, "Ten percent down and 30 years to pay."

Without even giving it much thought, the man exclaimed, "Where do I sign?"

In the last frame, the same man was talking to his pastor. The pastor asked him, "Would you please sign this commitment card to give the Lord 10 percent of your money for the next year?"

In shock and horror, the man replied, "What! And tie myself to an obligation like that for 52 weeks? No sir! The future is too insecure. I don't want to make a commitment that I might not be able to keep."

This man readily obligated himself for 48 months for a car, 12 months for a refrigerator, and 30 years for a house. But he didn't want to obligate himself to the Lord at all!

Now, I am not against buying a house or car on credit. I merely want to point out how quickly we agree to those kinds of terms, but when it comes to our giving to the Lord, we sometimes hold on to our money so tightly. It's a tragedy when God takes second place with our finances.

I heard another story about a wealthy man who died and went to Heaven. As he and Peter were walking down the streets of gold, they came to a beautiful mansion. The wealthy man exclaimed, "Ah, is that mine?"

"No," Peter replied. "That's not your home. Follow me and I'll take you to yours." So they walked on down the streets of gold and came to another place that was as beautiful as the first one.

The rich man sighed, "Oh, this must be mine."

"No," Peter said. "This isn't your place, but just follow me. It isn't far now."

So they rounded a bend and came upon a tiny shack, and Peter said to the man, "Here's your home."

The rich man was appalled! "You mean this tiny shack is my house for eternity?"

Peter looked at the man very patiently and said, "Well, I did the best I could with what you sent."

Let me ask you today, what kind of mansion are you going to have? What are you sending God to work with? Those are sobering questions, but we all need to answer them.

The Percentage Rule

When I was very young, my parents taught me about tithing. I learned at the age of three or four that if I received a dollar, ten cents of that dollar was supposed to go to the Lord. The percentage rule was instilled in my spirit long before I ever learned that principle at school.

I was taught that God blessed us, but we were supposed to give the tithe back to Him. That was always sacred to me, and I've followed that principle all of my life. It was never a question of *whether* I was going to tithe. The only question I asked was, "How much is my tithe this week?"

These days, people are holding on so tightly to their wallets. Many are thinking, *Well, I'd better save all I can.* And the first place they cut back on their spending is at church. But our giving to the Lord is the one place where we should never tighten our budgets!

Of course, Satan will do everything he can to try to stop you from tithing. Why? Because he knows the blessings you're going to receive when you tithe, and he loves to keep you from receiving God's blessings.

He'll tell you, "If you tithe, you won't have enough money to pay your bills." He'll threaten you by saying, "If you tithe, you're not going to be able to eat this week." As I mentioned previously, I have tithed all of my life, but I have never gone hungry, and I have always been able to pay my bills.

I'm so thankful my parents taught me to seek first the Kingdom of God and His righteousness and also to give my tithes and offerings to the Lord. They knew that following these biblical principles would cause me to prosper and be successful in life.

Write Your Tithe Check FIRST

I will never forget an incident that happened back in 1966, right after Ken and I were married. Our budget was really tight in those days, and it's always been my responsibility to pay the bills and make the budget work. In other words, I am the keeper of the books. But as I began to calculate what our expenses were going to be that month, I suddenly realized there wasn't enough money to meet all of our needs.

For the first time in my life, the thought crossed my mind, *You can hold back your tithes this month and make it up next month.* But because the principle of tithing had been so strongly instilled in me, I was able to say, "No, Satan, you're not going to cut off the very thing that's going to open the windows of Heaven for me!"

I told Ken about the situation, and we joined hands and agreed that our needs were going to be met. Then I wrote our tithe check and I told the Lord, "God, we're standing on Your Word and expecting You to meet every need."

There were times when I tried to figure out how God was going to help us pay all the bills. I watched for extra money to arrive in the mail, but we didn't receive any. No money dropped out of Heaven. No one handed us a special offering at church.

But what happened to us was similar to what happened to the widow at Zarephath in First Kings 17:8–16. If you remember the story, she first gave some of her meal and oil to make a cake for the prophet Elijah. As a result, every time she went to her meal barrel and cruse of oil, she had enough left over to make another meal. God supernaturally provided for her, as well as her son and the prophet, until the famine was over!

One by one, as the bills came in that month, I wrote the checks to pay them. And every time I wrote another check, there was just enough in our checking account to cover the need.

As God is my witness, at the end of the month I had paid every bill, we had not missed any meals, and we had $5 left in our bank account. I do not know where the money came from, but I can truthfully tell you that our God is able to supply all of our needs according to His riches in glory by Christ Jesus (Phil. 4:19)!

From that moment on, I told the Lord, "The first thing I'm going to do every month is write out my tithe check. Then I'm going to calculate the rest of my budget for the month." From that day to this, as soon as my pay is deposited in the bank, the very first check I write is for my tithe. And because I'm honoring God and putting Him first, He always supplies my needs.

Don't Eat Your Seed

The problem with many Christians today is that they are eating their seed. Think about a farmer. He may have a large amount of land to produce a crop. The soil may be extremely fertile. There may be abundant rain to help him produce a good crop. In other words, the farmer could have all the right conditions for a wonderful harvest.

Not only that, but the farmer could say all the right faith confessions. He could declare, "I thank You, Lord, that I have abundant land. I thank You that the soil is fertile and there's plenty of rain. I thank You for giving me a good crop." He can make all the confessions he wants to make, but until he puts some seed into the ground, he will not reap a harvest!

Many Christians today are saying all the right words. They're confessing: "Oh, I thank You, Father, that all of my needs are met. Thank You that I have more than enough.

Thank You that my cup is running over." They're making their faith confessions, but absolutely nothing is happening. Why? Those are empty faith confessions if they're not planting any seed!

Let's look at some verses in Second Corinthians chapter 9 on the subject of giving.

2 CORINTHIANS 9:6–8

6 But this I say, He which soweth sparingly shall reap also sparingly; and he which soweth bountifully shall reap also bountifully.

7 Every man according as he purposeth in his heart, so let him give; not grudgingly, or of necessity: for God loveth a cheerful giver.

8 And God is able to make all grace abound toward you; that ye, always having all sufficiency in all things, may abound to every good work.

In these verses God is giving us some clear instructions about our giving. We are not to give to the Lord with a grudging attitude—because we have to or just because He expects it. He doesn't want us to come to Him saying, "OK, God, here's my 10 percent. This is my $20.35—I've calculated it right down to the last penny."

No, the Lord wants us to bring our tithes and offerings to Him cheerfully, because it's such a privilege to give! He wants us to be thankful that He's blessed and prospered us so we *can* give.

Let's look at a verse in Luke chapter 6.

LUKE 6:38

38 Give, and it shall be given unto you; good measure, pressed down, and shaken together, and running over, shall men give into your bosom. For with the same measure that ye mete withal it shall be measured to you again.

The principle Jesus presented in Luke 6:38 is very simple. God wants us to give, and it shall be given back to us—good measure, pressed down, shaken together, and running over. I like that running-over part! Then the Lord said, " . . . *shall men give into your bosom.*"

To me, this subject is clear. If you don't like what you're reaping, check up on your sowing. You might say, "But I've been sowing, and it doesn't look like I'm reaping anything at all."

Then think about this for a moment. When a farmer plants a crop, he doesn't reap a harvest overnight, does he? But I guarantee you, if you keep on sowing, you will reap a harvest *in due season* (Gal. 6:9).

We must always remember that God is obligated to give us a harvest on the seeds we sow. He's obligated to perform what He promised in His Word.

In the days we're living in, I challenge you to honor God first with your finances. If you want Him to bless you and multiply the seed in your life, it's important for you to plant the seed that belongs to Him—your tithes and offerings. Then expect Him to multiply that seed back to you— exceedingly abundantly, above all that you can ask, think, or imagine (Eph. 3:20)!

You're Happier When You Give!

Do you realize that you're a much happier person when you give? I'm not just talking about the giving of your finances. You're happier when you're giving to God in any area of your life. You're happier when you're giving to others. In fact, the happiest people I know are those who give!

Sometimes we may ask ourselves, "If I give this money to the Lord, how will my needs be met?" But in many cases, God is faithfully meeting our needs and we don't even recognize it.

You see, God is blessing your life continually. He's giving you the strength to do your job. He's giving you the wisdom you need. He's giving you knowledge, opportunities, and promotions. Psalm 1:3 says that He causes whatever you do to prosper.

When I was pregnant with our son, Craig, we had no hospitalization insurance. So I told the Lord, "God, the cost of a hospital bill is not figured into our budget. We're paying our tithes and giving our offerings. We're doing what we know to do. And we're standing on Your Word that You're going to bring us the money to pay this medical bill."

Once again, the money didn't rain down on us from Heaven. No money came in the mail. No one gave us any special offerings. We didn't get a raise on our jobs.

But God gave us an opportunity. Someone in our church told us, "We have a new home construction business, and we need someone to put signs up to advertise our business. The signs have to be put up on Friday night, but they must be taken down on Sunday night. We'll pay you $100 a month if you're interested." That may not seem like a lot of money now, but it seemed like $1,000 a month to us back in 1969!

We were thrilled to get that offer. And that was the way God provided the finances to pay the hospital bill when our son was born. God may not answer our prayers the way we think He should. But He always answers. He always provides!

Many times a minister will try to hype you up about your giving so he can collect a large offering. But I'm not trying to hype you up about this subject. I *do* want to tell you what God has said in His Word. And I also want to remind you that you will be blessed when you obey what God impresses you in your heart to do.

Sometimes when preparing to receive an offering, someone will talk about the running-over blessing in Luke 6:38. When you hear about that running-over supply, you may be stirred in your heart to give. But if you're not careful, you may wind up giving more than you can actually afford to give. You give not only your tithes but more offerings than your budget allows. All of a sudden, you realize you've given foolishly. Thank God, the Lord doesn't want us to give foolishly!

I've also heard people say, "You need to sow your tithes on the amount you want to make." Now I'm not telling you this is wrong. But I *am* telling you that you have to start where you are. And I'm also giving you some simple, practical things you can do concerning your giving.

First of all, if you haven't started tithing, I encourage you to start giving your 10 percent to the Lord before you try to give any large offerings. Second, pray and seek the Lord concerning any offerings He desires for you to give.

Of course, there may be times when God leads us to give sacrificially. There have been times when my husband and I have been prompted by the Holy Spirit to give a sacrificial gift. There have also been times when we felt impressed in our spirits to give a certain amount as a seed for something we desired. Not long ago, we were impressed to give sacrificially for a specific desire we had, and do you know what? That desire came to pass!

I'm telling you, God will faithfully perform His Word. But the most important thing we can do is give to Him consistently and systematically. Just as you pay your bills every week or every two weeks, write out your tithe check regularly. As soon as you get paid, write your tithe check before you even figure your bills. I believe you'll find there will be not only enough, but there will be more than enough . . . because you're obeying God's Word and putting Him first!

God Is Our El Shaddai

The Body of Christ has a Great Commission to accomplish for the Lord in this hour. There is so much work that needs to be done in these last days. It's going to take each and every one of us giving our time, our talents, and our treasures—our money—to do what God has called us to do.

Are you willing to commit to giving God your treasures? Are you ready to plant some seed to Him? If you don't already tithe, I encourage you to make a dedication in your heart right now that you're going to do so. If you do tithe, I urge you to dedicate yourself to giving more offerings this year than you ever have before. And remember, God is going to bless you for it. When we come in line with His Word, what a mighty harvest we are going to reap!

Why? Because our Heavenly Father is El Shaddai, the God Who is more than enough. He's not just barely enough. He doesn't hand out His blessings in a miserly fashion!

He's the Abundant One—the God Who pours out on us His full and rich supply. And as we in the Body of Christ band together, giving of our time, our talents, our prayers, and our treasures, the lost will be saved, God's plan for this world will be accomplished, and nothing—absolutely nothing—will be impossible to us!

Chapter 14

~~~

LEAVING A LEGACY

Let me ask you a serious question: what kind of legacy are you leaving in life? Or I could put it this way: what kind of history book are you writing?

Whether we realize it or not, we're all writing our own history book—telling the story of our lives. We're all leaving a legacy for those around us to follow. The kind of legacy we leave is vitally important, because that's how we make our contribution to the world.

One definition of *legacy* is something "handed down from . . . an ancestor." In other words, it's something handed down from one generation to the next. This can include our traits, habits, and talents, and our attitudes—social, physical, mental, spiritual, and emotional.

Do you realize all the things you're handing down to your children and the others who are closest to you? Often our loved ones, especially the children in our lives, do certain things because they admire us and want to be like us.

I know when our oldest grandson, Cameron, was about 4, they were having trouble with him at the day care center. He just adores my husband, his Poppy. Poppy means everything to Cameron, and he's always tried to walk in Poppy's footsteps. But he got into trouble at the day care center because he imitated one of Poppy's habits!

You see, when my husband is outside, he has a habit of spitting on the ground. The day care teachers told us that Cameron was spitting on the floor in the classroom. Why was he doing that? He was imitating his Poppy! But he was having trouble discerning where to spit and where not to spit.

What is my point here? Many times we're writing a legacy that people are going to follow, whether we realize it or not. For example, my husband has certain mannerisms he picked up from his dad. Does he do those things on purpose? No. They're simply part of the legacy his father left him.

Let me ask you another question: How do you want others to remember you? Do you want to be known for how intelligent or well-educated you are? Do you want people to remember how well-dressed or well-organized you are or how much "bling" you have? Remember, you're developing the legacy right now that you will leave behind for others to follow.

A story told about Louis Pasteur, known as the father of immunology, illustrates this well. Pasteur was working on a vaccine for rabies during a period when there was a terrible outbreak of that disease. A 10-year-old boy named Joseph Meister was bitten by a dog and contracted rabies. Because there was no cure at the time, it appeared he was going to die.

His mother begged Pasteur to help them, saying, "Just try that antidote you've been developing on my son. He's going to die anyway." Pasteur gave in and administered the treatment to the boy. Shortly after that, he began to amend. The epidemic was doomed and Joseph Meister's life was spared.

Near the end of Pasteur's life, he wrote his own epitaph. As he formulated the statement that would adorn his tomb, he resisted the temptation to use a lengthy list of his honors and accomplishments. Instead, this is what he wanted to have engraved on his tombstone: "Joseph Meister lived." You see, the real measure of a person's success lies not in accomplishments, awards, or degrees, but in the lives that have been changed because of his or her influence.

Leaving the Right Example

You may never realize all the people who are watching you. Having grown up in a minister's home, I've been aware all of my life that people were probably watching me. It's an awesome responsibility to make sure that you're giving them the right example to follow.

Think of some of the people who have influenced your life. The first person who comes to my mind when I think about those who have influenced me is Granny King, my mother's mother. I dearly loved my Granny King. She always took time to be with her grandchildren. I especially remember how she loved to take us to the zoo.

Now Granny King didn't drive, and sometimes Paw-Paw wasn't too happy about having to drive us kids to the zoo. But Granny was always insistent. Granny and Paw-Paw didn't have a lot of money to spend on us, but they were careful to spend their time with us.

Granny King had one precious possession—her little coin purse. She always had her coin purse with her. Even though they didn't have much money, I remember her giving us grandchildren a few coins when we visited her. After Granny died, my mother asked me, "What would you like to have that belonged to her?" The only thing I wanted was her coin purse.

My memories of Granny King have helped me realize the importance of spending time with my own children. Although we were busy in the ministry when our children were growing up, I knew we needed to spend time having fun with them. And we needed to do that not only with our children, but also with our grandchildren.

Not long ago my husband and I took all five of our grandsons on a vacation together. Five boys! One thing it made me realize was how thankful I am that we did not have five boys!

We went to amusement parks, and the boys had fun while Ken and I made memories. Really, it was fun for us, too, but it was also work. One reason we do things like that is, my grandmother left a legacy by taking time with her grandchildren.

Another person who had a tremendous influence on my life was my first-grade teacher—Mrs. Fletcher. Now it's important for you to understand that Mrs. Fletcher was my *third* first-grade teacher. You see, I attended three different schools during my first-grade year!

It had been a traumatic experience for me to leave my mother and go to school in the first place. But you can imagine how I felt, having to go to three different schools in one year. That's why Mrs. Fletcher's kindness meant so much to me.

I have a picture of our class that year that I will always treasure. In it, I'm standing right next to Mrs. Fletcher, and she has her hand on my shoulder. I was a little insecure by the time I enrolled in her class. But she would always pat me on the shoulder and say, "It's going to be okay, honey."

I know it was because of Mrs. Fletcher that I passed that first year. It was also because she took an interest in an insecure little girl that I developed a love and desire to help children as well as grown-ups who feel insecure.

You see, she was passing on to me a legacy that I still practice every day of my life. When I'm at an event and I see someone who is uncomfortable with strangers, I try to connect them with someone who can talk to anybody. I love to make insecure people feel secure. Why? Because of the legacy left to me by Mrs. Fletcher.

Then I remember my fifth-grade teacher, Mrs. Glaze. She was a short, jolly little lady who was always smiling. I never saw Mrs. Glaze downcast or having a bad day. She loved to laugh and have fun.

Mrs. Glaze was extremely good for me because I came from a very serious family. My family members were all workaholics, and I had never been taught how to laugh and have fun.

So Mrs. Glaze gave me a wonderful legacy by helping me learn how to laugh and have a good time. Little did I know how important that was going to be in life, but God knew. He said in Proverbs 17:22, "*A merry heart doeth good like a medicine. . . .*" Our Heavenly Father knows how important it is for us to laugh and enjoy life!

Precious Memories

I have a Bible in my home that's very precious to me because it belonged to my dear Aunt Oma. That Bible is so worn and tattered that I hardly ever lift it or move it around because I'm afraid it might fall to pieces!

Why does that Bible mean so much to me? Aunt Oma is the one who taught me the importance of the Word of God and prayer. She taught me that all you had to do was ask your Heavenly Father for whatever you needed and He would answer you. And I can certainly testify that Aunt Oma always got her prayers answered!

Sometimes ~~I tell people that God answered Aunt Oma~~'s ~~prayers because He got tired of her bugging Him.~~ But whatever the case, her prayers were always answered. And she's the one who taught me to persevere in prayer. I will forever be grateful for her legacy in my life.

When I was a little girl, Aunt Oma would say to me, "Honey, why don't you come over to my house. I want you to learn some scriptures." How many 5-year-olds do you know who would be willing to sit there, hour after hour, and memorize scriptures? I would recite those verses over and over again as Aunt Oma helped me develop a strong love for the Word of God.

I'm so thankful that Aunt Oma instilled those Bible verses in my heart, because they've helped me know what to do when the tough times came. The legacy Aunt Oma left gave me a strong assurance that my God would always be there for me, in good times and bad.

I also remember the things my precious dad taught me. He went home to be with the Lord in 2002 at the age of 89. My dad taught me the joy of giving to others. You see, Daddy lived to give. And he also taught me compassion, because he was always so compassionate toward others.

He gave of himself, but he also loved to give of his finances. Our kids still remember one Fourth of July when they were visiting my dad and mom. He told them, "OK, kids, we're going to buy some fireworks so we can shoot them off at the lake." Then he told them to pick out some fireworks.

They didn't get enough to suit him, so he urged them, "Go and get some more!" Very politely, they chose a few more. But he insisted, "No, that's not enough. Get some more." So they chose a few more fireworks, but Daddy still wasn't satisfied. He was such a generous giver that he insisted on buying them even more fireworks!

Not only was Daddy a giving person, but he also taught me to have a strong work ethic. He taught me never to give up. And he encouraged me to think before I spoke. He always said, "The words you say cannot be recaptured. Be careful what you say."

One of the most important things I remember about my daddy is that he was always there for me. He was my encourager, and I'm so thankful for that. I will always be grateful for the legacy my dad passed on to me.

A Mother's Legacy

When I think about all the things my mother taught me, I remember most of all how she showed me by her example how to be a colaborer with my husband in the ministry. She taught me how to take my place by my husband's side, to complement him and not compete with him. She showed me how to be his helpmate, and I'm deeply grateful for that.

In the natural arena, Mother told me, "Lynette, you should always set a beautiful table, even if it's only for your family." To this day, my mother still puts out the placemats, even if it's just the two of us eating together. And she still sets the table with her china and silver.

My mother also taught me how to cook and be a good wife to my husband. I'm thankful for her godly example and the legacy she has left me.

And then there's the tremendous legacy I received from my father-in-law and mother-in-law. My father-in-law taught me, "having done all, to stand" (Eph. 6:13). He showed me how to believe God in spite of any circumstances I may encounter. Of course, he instructed me about faith, but even more than that, he taught me how to forgive and walk in love. I will forever be grateful for all the things he instilled in my life.

The most important thing my mother-in-law taught me is how to stand by your man. She taught me that the price is not greater than God's grace. Many stories were related over the years of how they didn't have much, and yet she always stood by her man.

I have to say that I am extremely grateful to my mother-in-law for teaching her son not to clutter the house. She taught him to hang up his clothes. She even encouraged him to help clean the house. I am forever thankful for that because I can truthfully say I have never had to hang up one stitch of clothing for my husband. I have never had to clean up any of his messes. That's because of the legacy left to him by his mother.

As my mother-in-law told me good-bye right before she went home to be with the Lord, she said to me, "Lynette, you've been such a good wife to my son. Thank you so much." Then she said something else I will never forget. She said, "Lynette, you and I have never had a cross word." I hadn't even thought about it. You always hear terrible stories about the conflicts between mothers-in-law and daughters-in-law, but it doesn't have to be that way. I'm so thankful for the legacy my mother-in-law has left in our lives.

Your Personal Legacy

Now I want to share some things that we all need to pass on in our personal legacy. First of all, we need to pass on the legacy of a life that has been lived for God. Judges 2:10 says, *"After that whole generation had been gathered to their fathers, another generation grew up, who knew neither the Lord nor what he had done for Israel"* (NIV). That tells me that if we're not careful to leave the proper legacy, we're going to have a whole generation who knows nothing about the Lord.

It's startling to read some of the statistics that describe the dramatic drop over the past few decades in the number of people who profess to be Christians. We have a huge job to do if we want the younger generation to grow spiritually. We must pass on our spiritual heritage, and I'm not merely talking about our acceptance of Jesus Christ as our Savior. I'm talking about living a life that's truly committed to the Lord.

The spiritual legacy my parents left me can be summed up in one verse—Matthew 6:33: "*Seek ye first the kingdom of God, and his righteousness; and all these things shall be added unto you.*"

My parents taught me that the most important value in life is seeking God first. That meant going to church when I didn't feel like going. It meant volunteering in the church when I really didn't want to volunteer. It meant listening to sermons that as a young person I didn't particularly enjoy. But my parents assured me, "Honey, you'll get something out of this if you'll just listen."

I appreciate my parents teaching me to love and respect God and the ministry and put the Lord first. They taught me that if I would give God first place, He would take care of all the other things.

When times have been difficult, I've always been able to rely on the things my parents instilled in me. Above all, they showed me how important it is to leave a legacy of a life lived for the Lord.

A Legacy of Respect and Honor

The second thing we must include in our personal legacy is teaching our children to respect their elders and live a life of honor. What has happened to ethics in our day? What has happened to showing appreciation and honor to those who are older than we are?

We live in a culture that promotes youthfulness. They want to cast out the aged, and they don't think they can learn anything from older people. But Leviticus 19:32 says, " *'Rise in the presence of the aged, show respect for the elderly and revere your God . . .'* " (NIV).

Really, I believe the root of many of the problems in the world today is that parents have not taught their children to obey and honor them. The first commandment I was taught was, *"Children, obey your parents in the Lord . . . for this is just and right"* (Eph. 6:1 Amplified). The next verse says, *"Honor (esteem and value as precious) your father and your mother— this is the first commandment with a promise."*

I was taught to obey my parents and respect the older generation. I was assured that I could learn from them. You can learn a lot from people who are older than you are, and it can save you many heartaches.

Not only that, but we older people can learn from younger people. I remember my Aunt Lella asking me for my opinion about something when I was only 13 years old.

I felt really insecure at the time, and when Aunt Lella asked for my opinion, I was shocked! She was in her 60s, and yet she was asking a 13-year-old for her opinion.

So I gave her my opinion, but then I said, "Aunt Lella, why on earth would you ask for a 13-year-old's opinion when I'm sure you're much more capable than I am of having the right opinion on this subject?"

"Honey," she replied, "it doesn't matter how old you are. We can always learn from those who are younger than us." That was a good lesson for me, and it's part of the legacy Aunt Lella left for me. She helped me realize that I can learn from others, no matter what their age!

A Life of Character

The third thing we must pass on in our personal legacy is a life of character. The impression we leave with others is not based upon our accomplishments but our character. Living out our integrity is what will have a lasting effect on others.

Character is doing right when no one else is looking. It's being honest, compassionate, and forgiving. It means being a person of your word and someone who puts others first. What are you recording in your history book about your character?

When I think of character, I think about the story of the three Hebrew children in Daniel chapter 3. The king said, "If you don't bow, you're going to be thrown into my burning, fiery furnace."

But they replied, "O king, we're not careful to answer you. Our God is able to deliver us. But even if He doesn't, we're not going to bow down to your gods." That was their character talking. And that's the kind of legacy we need to leave for the next generation.

The fourth thing we need to pass on to those who will come after us is the legacy of a life of faith in God. Are you passing on your faith to your children and those who are close to you? Psalm 78:4 says, *"We will not hide these truths from our children; we will tell the next generation about the glorious deeds of the Lord, about his power and his mighty wonders"* (NLT).

Are you telling your children the great Bible stories about the men and women who lived by their faith in God? Are you telling them about Daniel in the lions' den, David and Goliath, and Esther, who had "come to the kingdom for such a time as this" (Esther 4:14)?

Are you teaching your children how to use their faith so they will know that they can do all things through Christ who strengthens them (Phil. 4:13)? Are you telling them that the things which are impossible with men are possible with God (Luke 18:27)? What kind of history book are you writing? What kind of legacy are you leaving for those who will follow you?

Write the New Pages!

You may be thinking, *Lynette, the history book I've already written isn't a very good one. I've made a mess of my life. I haven't written the right pages in my personal legacy.*

I have good news for you! You can start fresh. You can write new pages in your history book. You can make a new commitment to the Lord that you're going to leave a legacy that will make a difference in someone's life!

I encourage you to pray this prayer from your heart:

Father, I commit to You now that I will leave the right kind of legacy for others to follow—a legacy that will lead them down the right path, and that will help them stand in the trying times of life.

I surrender my all to You, O Lord, to follow in Your way and live a life consecrated to You. May I live a life of honor, a life of integrity, a life of character, and a life of faith in You. May I always extend my hand to those who are in need. May I practice love, kindness, forgiveness, and restoration. May I always speak words of love.

Heavenly Father, I ask You to forgive me for the times I've spoken harshly. Forgive me when I haven't shown Your love to others. Help me follow You in all of my ways and let my example be one that others will be blessed to follow. In Jesus' Name I pray, amen.

This is a new day—a new era! You're about to embark upon some new things that God has planned for you. That means you can begin writing a new legacy—a new history book—today!

Remember, Paul said in Philippians 3:13–14, "*Brethren, I count not myself to have apprehended: but this one thing I do, forgetting those things which are behind, and reaching forth unto those things which are before, I press toward the mark for the prize of the high calling of God in Christ Jesus.*"

God doesn't want us to focus on the past anymore. He has greater things for us to accomplish in the future. He has awesome plans for those of us who will stand firm in the things of the Lord. He has a greater history book for us to write!

He has set the blank pages before you. As you fill those pages, I want you to think about the legacy you're leaving for your precious children and other loved ones. As they look at your history book—your legacy—will it help them fulfill the plan God has for their lives? Will it be a legacy they can follow to win their race in life?

I believe it's time for you to make your mark—your contribution to the world. May it always be said in your history book that you have made a difference in someone else's life!

...uld you consider attending
RHEMA
...le Training Center?

Here are a few good reasons:

- Training at one of the top Spirit-filled Bible schools anywhere
- Teaching based on steadfast faith in God's Word
- Growth in your spiritual walk coupled with practical training in effective ministry
- Specialization in the area of your choosing: Youth or Children's Ministry, Evangelism, Pastoral Care, Missions, Biblical Studies, or Supportive Ministry
- Optional intensive third-year programs: School of Worship, School of Pastoral Ministry, School of World Missions, and General Extended Studies
- Worldwide ministry opportunities—while you're in school
- An established network of churches and ministries around the world who depend on RHEMA to supply full-time staff and support ministers
- A two-year evening school taught entirely in Spanish is also available. Log on to **www.cebrhema.org** for more information.

Call today for information or application material.
1-888-28-FAITH (1-888-283-2484)
www.rbtc.org

RHEMA Bible Training Center admits students of any race, color, or ethnic origin.

OFFER CODE—BKORD:PRMDRBTC

Always on.

For the latest news and information on products, media, podcasts, study resources, and special offers, visit us online 24 hours a day.